Improving School Leadership
The Promise of Cohesive Leadership Systems

Catherine H. Augustine · Gabriella Gonzalez · Gina Schuyler Ikemoto · Jennifer Russell
Gail L. Zellman · Louay Constant · Jane Armstrong · Jacob W. Dembosky

Commissioned by

The Wallace Foundation

Supporting ideas.
Sharing solutions.
Expanding opportunities.

RAND EDUCATION

The research in this report was produced within RAND Education, a division of the RAND Corporation, and was commissioned by The Wallace Foundation.

Library of Congress Cataloging-in-Publication Data

Improving school leadership : the promise of cohesive leadership systems / Catherine H.
  Augustine ... [et al.].
    p. cm.
  "This study was conducted by RAND Education"—Pref.
  Includes bibliographical references.
  ISBN 978-0-8330-4891-2 (pbk. : alk. paper)
  1. Educational leadership—United States. 2. School management and
organization—United States. 3. Educational change—United States. 4. School
principals—United States. 5. Public schools—United States. 6. Education and
state—United States. I. Augustine, Catherine H., 1968– II. Rand Education
(Institute)

LB2805.I4367 2010
371.200973—dc22

2009045738

Published 2009 by the RAND Corporation
1776 Main Street, P.O. Box 2138, Santa Monica, CA 90407-2138
1200 South Hayes Street, Arlington, VA 22202-5050
4570 Fifth Avenue, Suite 600, Pittsburgh, PA 15213-2665
RAND URL: http://www.rand.org/
To order RAND documents or to obtain additional information, contact
Distribution Services: Telephone: (310) 451-7002;
Fax: (310) 451-6915; Email: order@rand.org

Preface

Recent research has identified the importance of school leadership in improving outcomes for schools and their students. For the past nine years, The Wallace Foundation has been providing funding and technical assistance to state and district grantees to help them work together to create a "cohesive leadership system" of policies and initiatives to improve educational leadership. The Foundation commissioned the RAND Corporation to document what its grantees have done with this support, to describe the strategies they have used to develop cohesive systems, and to examine the theory that more-cohesive systems improve school leadership.

This monograph is intended primarily for those who are concerned with improving school leadership, including state education agencies, chief state school officers, professional standards boards, postsecondary education governing bodies, professional associations, and leaders of public schools and districts. It may also be of interest to other policymakers and practitioners who wish to strengthen the collaboration between state and district education officials to improve public education.

This study was conducted by RAND Education, a unit of the RAND Corporation. The work was supported by The Wallace Foundation, which for two decades has been dedicated to enabling institutions to expand learning and enrichment opportunities for all people. The Foundation carries out its mission by funding the development and testing of new ideas, capturing and sharing lessons from these endeavors, and commissioning related independent research. It currently works chiefly in three areas: strengthening education leadership to improve student achievement, enhancing out-of-school-time learning opportunities, and building appreciation of and demand for the arts.

Contents

Figures

Tables

Summary

Improving the nation's public schools is one of the highest priorities of America's federal, state, and local governments. Among the imperatives gaining attention in recent years is the need to develop school leaders who are capable of exercising more vigilance over instruction and developing an institutional culture that supports effective teaching practices. To catalyze improvements in student learning, many states have enacted new leadership standards for principals and revised criteria for leader training programs. Districts, too, have begun to pay more heed to their own human resource pipelines by establishing programs to train aspiring principals and to develop the skills of mid-career principals. Recent research supports these efforts by finding that the quality of the principal is, among school-based factors, second only to the quality of the teacher in contributing to what students learn in the classroom (Leithwood et al., 2004).

These achievements, however, are not likely to have their desired effect if new policies and initiatives are inconsistent with other state and district policies affecting school leadership. If, for example, new leadership standards are implemented by the state but fail to influence the curriculum of professional preparation programs, they will have only marginal impact. And if principals receive strong leadership training aligned with standards but find that they have little authority over their school budgets or hiring, they will not be able to put the best practices they have learned into effect at their schools.

The Wallace Foundation, which has focused its grantmaking in education primarily on school leadership, has long recognized the need for more-coordinated state and district policies in this area. The Foundation's grants to states and districts over the past nine years have been designed to overcome the isolation of targeted reforms and to forge policy connections that could lead to more-cohesive and high-performing systems. The working hypothesis, or theory of action, behind these investments is that a cohesive leadership system (CLS), defined as well-coordinated policies and initiatives across state agencies and between the state and its districts, will increase the ability of principals to improve instruction in their schools. In particular, the hypothesis holds that coordinating the development of leadership standards, high-quality training, and the conditions that affect principals' work (such as access to data and sufficient resources) will facilitate successful school leadership and support improved teaching and student learning. The Foundation commissioned RAND to document the results of its initiative and in the process to examine this hypothesis.

Study Purpose and Approach

This study had three objectives:

1. To document the actions taken by Wallace Foundation grantees to create a more cohesive set of policies and initiatives to improve instructional leadership in schools
2. To describe how states and districts have worked together to forge more-cohesive policies and initiatives around school leadership
3. To examine the hypothesis that more-cohesive systems do in fact improve school leadership.

To document what the grantees at selected sites had accomplished, the RAND research team addressed three questions:

1. What policies and initiatives have states and districts pursued to improve school leadership?
2. How are the states and districts interacting to improve school leadership?
3. To what extent have they built cohesion among school leadership policies and initiatives?

To describe system development, we addressed several other questions, including, What strategies have sites used to build CLSs and why are some sites more cohesive than others? And how are sites attempting to scale up and sustain their work?

The third objective—examining The Wallace Foundation's hypothesis—proved to be a difficult analytic challenge. Linking improved cohesion with student outcomes was beyond the scope of this two-year project. We chose instead to focus on the link between the conditions within which principals work and their reports on (and satisfaction with) time spent on specific instructional practices.

We performed a cross-case analysis, using a purposive sample of 10 Wallace grantee sites consisting of 10 states and their 17 affiliated districts. Before conducting site visits, we reviewed the literature on system-building and policy coherence and developed an understanding of the indicators of cohesive systems that we used to structure, compare, and interpret our findings. We then conducted site visits during which we interviewed 300 representatives of districts, state government, and pre-service principal preparation programs. We also fielded a survey of more than 600 principals and collected information in an online log in which nearly 170 principals described how they spent their time every day for two weeks. We supplemented this information by interviewing 100 principals.

Results

The study found that it is possible to build more-cohesive leadership systems and that such efforts appear to be a promising approach to developing school leaders engaged in improving instruction. Perhaps the most useful result of the analysis is our account of the strategies state and district actors have devised to build stronger working relationships and greater cohesion around policies and initiatives to improve education. By identifying those sites that had built more-cohesive systems, we were able to compare their strategies and historical contexts with those of sites that had not yet achieved fully cohesive systems. In this way, we were able to identify effective approaches to this work and local conditions that fostered success. These findings should be useful to others building statewide systems to improve education. Although we could not provide evidence that the full underlying theory behind the Wallace initiative is sound, we did find a correlation between improved conditions for principals and their engagement in instructional practices.

What Are States and Districts Doing to Improve School Leadership?

Policies and initiatives. All the study sites had done something to improve school leadership. Their efforts were focused on six areas: standards, pre-service and recruitment, licensure, evaluation, in-service, and the conditions in which principals work. The policies and initiatives differed across sites in their focus, scope, stage of implementation, and the degree to which they challenged the status quo. We found that states and districts were equally likely to be engaged in this work. We also found that state and district domains of responsibility were converging. For example, states we studied were mandating evaluation systems and professional development for principals, which used to be primarily the domain of districts. Conversely, districts were developing their own pre-service programs (on their own, in partnership with local universities, or in partnership with nontraditional providers), a domain once dominated by state government.

Roles and interactions. We observed two patterns of interaction across the sites. In one, districts were, for the most part, improving school leadership on their own, without support or intervention from the state. In the other, the state was clearly the leader, with districts involved in primarily reactive ways. Kentucky was an exception; there, the school district and the state were equal partners in improving school leadership at the district and state levels. In Kentucky, and in some other sites falling into one of the two patterns above, the state was adept at identifying, supporting, and spreading good practices that were developed at the district level.

Degree of cohesion. We use the term *cohesion* to describe systems built in concert by the state and its affiliated districts. We identified sites with more- and less-advanced CLSs so that we could determine which strategies and contexts seemed to be beneficial in this work. Our analysis of interview data indicated that three sites—Delaware, Iowa, and Kentucky—had the most advanced CLSs at the time of our research. Compared with other sites, they exhibited all five characteristics we identified as present in highly cohesive leadership systems: comprehensiveness in the scope of their initiatives, alignment of policies and practices, broad stakeholder engagement, agreement on how to improve leadership, and coordination achieved through strong leadership. We also determined that although districts and states were equally likely to be taking action to improve leadership, states tended to lead efforts to build CLSs.

How Have Sites Built Cohesive Leadership Systems?

States, rather than districts, have played the key role in creating connections among state and district policies and initiatives on leadership. State agencies are better positioned than districts to foster broad stakeholder engagement and agreement among stakeholders, coordinate initiatives, and ensure statewide alignment of resulting policies. Organizations with a statewide purview are also more aware of other education reforms and how leadership improvements can be integrated into the broader agenda. A comparison of lead organizations, strategies, and contextual factors highlighted some important differences among state efforts.

Organizations leading efforts. Sites differed a great deal in the organizations that assumed the lead role in developing cohesiveness. In some sites, it was the state education agency (SEA); in others, it was a university or a professional association; in still others, a large district was an equal partner in the work. There appeared to be no "best" approach: The appropriate constellation of actors depended on the local context, including who had the power, capacity, and inclination to move the work forward.

In the sites with more-cohesive systems (Delaware, Iowa, and Kentucky), the lead agency was chosen strategically. For example, state leaders assessed the internal capacity of their own SEAs, taking into account whether staff would be able to think and work outside the boundaries created by categorical federal programs and the overall credibility of the SEA and its political priorities. These sites proactively developed distributed systems of leadership with key roles assigned to different types of organizations, including SEAs, universities, leadership academies, professional associations, regional education offices, and districts.

Strategies used to build cohesion. Interview data suggested that eight strategies were the most important for building cohesion:

1. Building trust
2. Creating formal and informal networks
3. Fostering communications

4. Exerting pressure and influence
5. Promoting improved quality of leadership policies and initiatives
6. Building capacity for the work
7. Identifying strong individuals with political and social capital to lead the work
8. Connecting to other reform efforts.

The sites with the most-cohesive leadership systems shared several distinctive approaches to implementing these strategies. First, unlike other sites, they were pursuing all eight strategies and working more intensively than others on three strategies in particular: building organizational capacity to accomplish the work, identifying leaders with strong social and political capital, and connecting the efforts on leadership improvement to other reform efforts in the state. Leaders who can connect school leadership reforms with other education initiatives in their states help build sustainability for their efforts and may reduce burdens on districts and schools. Also, in Delaware, Iowa, and Kentucky, distributed leadership systems were built with key state-level organizations, as described above.

Second, leaders in these states pursued strategic communications. Delaware and Iowa routinely gathered key state and district leaders into the same room to both learn about leadership and develop policies and initiatives to improve it. Kentucky accomplished the same goals in a serial fashion by holding town hall meetings throughout the state that were credited with creating "learning systems for leadership."

Third, all three sites combined pressure tactics and support in effective ways. In Kentucky, for example, to create an incentive for all higher education institutions to engage in pre-service redesign, Jefferson County Public Schools (JCPS) and the Department of Education sought approval from the State Board of Education to design their own program, applying pressure that succeeded in making the universities more active partners in the process. But Kentucky did not rely on pressure alone: CLS leaders also offered support for the redesign process in a number of ways.

Contextual factors that promoted or hindered the work. Interviewees reported a range of factors that enabled or inhibited efforts to build cohesion:

Enabling factors
- Common structures and policies
- A history of collaboration
- Strong preexisting social networks
- Participation of nontraditional actors
- Funding and technical assistance from The Wallace Foundation
- Political support
- Supportive, stable, and aligned superintendents and school boards

Inhibiting factors
- Limited resources
- Limited SEA capacity
- Turnover of key staff
- Too many organizations, too far apart
- Cultures of independence
- Discord across organizations
- Reform overload

Sites with the strongest record in building cohesion shared a number of enabling factors and were less limited by inhibiting factors. Delaware and Iowa both had a history of relatively positive relationships among deeply networked state-level stakeholders, as well as a history of collaboration among them. Although Kentucky did not have a history of positive collaboration between state and district actors, the Wallace funding and technical assistance created the opportunity for leaders from the SEA and JCPS to work collaboratively.

These sites also enjoyed a higher and more consistent level of political support than other sites in our sample. All three states have a history of activism in education reform, and their political leaders have long shared a commitment to school reform which created fertile ground for leadership initiatives.

Finally, the three sites were collectively less likely to face some of the key barriers to building a cohesive system, such as staff turnover, a culture of independence, or discord across organizations. Other barriers, however, were present, including limited resources and SEA capacity, organizations that were geographically far apart, and, in the case of Kentucky, a history of discord across organizations. We found some evidence that these three sites were more resourceful than others in developing strategies to overcome contextual challenges such as limited SEA capacity and a history of discord. Less-cohesive sites showed more limited capacity—and perhaps more limited will—to overcome such obstacles.

Sustaining and scaling up the work. Our interviews suggested that in more-cohesive sites, the CLS initiative is likely to continue beyond the period of Foundation support. Although many interviewees described challenges to sustaining this work once funding and technical assistance ends—challenges such as insufficient time, staff, and resources and the eventual loss of dynamic leaders—they also described creative strategies they were adopting to sustain and build on their achievements, including passing legislation, embedding the initiative into their state's education agenda, and vesting future leadership of the initiative in organizations outside government to help shield it from political changes in SEAs.

Many interviewees felt that their success in creating cohesion provided in itself some assurance that the initiative would survive. In some states, leaders felt their efforts had reached the point of no return: They had established bonds among people and agencies, a common language and vision, and widespread commitment to the goal of improving school leadership.

Did We Find Support for the CLS Hypothesis?

We were not able to determine whether more-cohesive systems were correlated with the ability of principals to spend more time on practices that are reported to be effective in improving the quality of instruction. However, we did find that principals reporting favorable conditions also reported that they spent more time on a series of instructional leadership practices. Our analysis does not provide evidence of causation—there could be other explanations for this correlation—nor can we demonstrate that principals spending more time on these practices has improved student learning. But our findings do offer some support for the theory that positive conditions for principals promote stronger instructional leadership.

Recommendations

Our study findings provide some practical lessons drawn from the experiences of the hundreds of people we interviewed. Although we focus on lessons learned about system-building to improve school leadership, our recommendations are intended to be helpful to anyone engaged in developing closer working relationships between states and districts that can result in better aligned policies for improving education.

Early Steps

Consider local contexts and address the challenges they pose. Our analysis showed that local context can work either for or against efforts to develop cohesion. Clearly, sites with a culture and history of collaboration and strong social networks are better suited for such efforts. A supportive political structure for public education reform is also important. We found that building cohesive systems under challenging conditions, such as limited resources, cultures of independence, or reform "burnout," was difficult. However, some sites found ways to surmount barriers. Other sites interested in emulating these reform efforts could closely examine their context and their capacity for them. In particular, they may want to address potential barriers before launching new reform efforts.

Identify strong lead organizations and individuals. Although lead agencies in the sites we studied varied, what the most advanced sites had in common—and what distinguished them from most others—was a strategic approach to the selection of people and organizations to lead the work. It is critical to find strong leaders who can form significant bases of power, garner political support for improving school leadership, and connect school leadership efforts to broader reform initiatives in the state. We recommend that sites determine which of their agencies or organizations is best poised to lead the effort to develop a CLS. In particular, sites should question whether the SEA is the best choice for this role, factoring in its overall capacity and credibility and its willingness to think and work outside the boundaries created by categorical federal programs.

Capitalize on external funding and expertise. All of the sites we studied benefited from funding and technical assistance from The Wallace Foundation. However, we found that many of the sites also capitalized on diverse sources of funding, such as local foundations, both before and during the course of the Wallace funding. They also sought technical assistance from others; all of the sites engaged external organizations, such as the Southern Regional Education Board (SREB), and key experts in school leadership to help them develop their capacity to do this work. The sites also met with each other to discuss strategies for success. Although securing a level of funding similar to the amounts awarded to the Wallace grantees may be challenging, new sites could investigate local foundations and businesses as possible sources. Furthermore, the sites described in this monograph are willing to provide technical assistance and guidance to other sites embarking on this work. Prospective sites could also learn from engaging expert organizations such as The Wallace Foundation and SREB as they explore options for building more-cohesive leadership systems.

The Implementation Phase

Build trust and mend fences. Relationships between state and district actors are sometimes acrimonious. The sites we studied reported that certain approaches to building trust were useful; such approaches included acknowledging that the state and the districts were "in this together" and ensuring that state actors took the time to understand district contexts and to develop the capacity to provide useful technical assistance. A "fresh face" also had benefits: New state actors repaired previously broken relationships between district and state organizations. Sites may need to address possible trust issues before undertaking efforts to develop CLSs. Once trust has been established, it should be easier to develop common understandings, shared goals, and joint ownership of the work.

Engage a broad coalition of stakeholders. Building cohesion requires serious efforts to engage stakeholders and foster agreement. Engagement for coordination requires time and resources. Sites should recognize the importance of involving relevant stakeholders and giving them the authority to make decisions, thereby fostering buy-in. Key state and district leaders would also benefit from meeting in the same room to discuss leadership and to develop policies and initiatives for improving it.

Hone skills at applying pressure while providing support. The most successful sites in this study combined pressure with support. This strategy benefited both states and districts. Applying pressure was effective when people perceived the state as willing and able to exercise its powers, and offering support was effective only when state actors and agencies could provide expertise that districts needed. Sites that can apply pressure while being supportive might accomplish the greatest policy reforms.

Recognize innovative districts as "lead learners." A number of innovative and sustainable policies and initiatives that began in the districts we studied spread to other districts and/or to state policy. States whose districts have made progress in improving school leadership should recognize these achievements and hold the districts up as possible models for others. State officials would benefit from partnering with such "lead learners" and creating mechanisms for scaling up relevant initiatives.

Connect school leadership efforts to standards and to other reforms in the state. Savvy leaders we interviewed knew how to link their efforts to build CLSs to other reforms in their states, such as high school and middle school reform programs. This approach helped to provide a platform from which to align policies and initiatives and appeared to foster both viability and sustainability. To bolster the success of leadership efforts, new sites could integrate leadership policies with other educational reforms in their districts and state.

Evaluation, Sustainment, and Expansion

Solidify programs and funding through legislation and regulations. Widespread and long-term reform was achieved through legislation and mandates that ensured that initiatives such as mentoring, evaluation systems, and the redesign of pre-service programs were implemented and funded. Other sites could include regulatory and funding designs in their efforts to build cohesion.

Engage in continuous learning and improvement. Leaders and organizations involved in building a CLS sought and shared expertise by participating in networks, attending conferences, and sharing ideas from research. They collected data to demonstrate that building a CLS had made a difference and to attract future funding. Other sites would benefit from similar commitments to continuous improvements.

Commit to engaging in this work over the long term. As many people told us, aligning policies and practices and building collaborative relationships between states and districts is hard work. Four of our study sites had been able to implement only a few initiatives despite receiving levels of funding and support similar to those of other, more successful sites. Even leaders in sites that have relatively advanced CLSs reported that only after nine years of effort were they beginning to see a real difference. Those who choose to embark on such an initiative should be prepared to engage in the work over the long term.

Final Thoughts

We found that it is possible to develop cohesive leadership systems between states and districts to improve school leadership, and we have identified the approaches that appear most effective for developing such systems, as well as local conditions that create a favorable environment for this work. Although we did not attempt to prove the hypothesis that such systems improve student outcomes, we affirmed the link between principals' conditions and the time they spend on instructional leadership practices. It is our hope that this analysis will help guide other states and districts in working collaboratively toward the common goal of improving school leadership.

Acknowledgments

Many people helped in conducting this study and producing this monograph. We would like to thank those at The Wallace Foundation for their substantive assistance and financial support. In particular, Mary Mattis provided valuable guidance on the intellectual and analytic components of our study. She and others reviewed draft documents and gave us incredibly valuable feedback and suggestions.

The Wallace Foundation's grantees of record were extremely helpful in identifying and enabling access to those persons most knowledgeable about the leadership improvement initiatives in each state and district. We are particularly grateful for the time given to us by our interviewees—both the experts we interviewed when we launched this project and those we interviewed at each site. Although we are keeping their identities confidential, their insights, opinions, and ideas formed the basis of our study.

Neil DeWeese and Stephanie Lonsinger coordinated the survey work, scheduled interviews across the sites, and edited and fact-checked contributions. Diana Epstein, Scott Epstein, Maxine Klimasara, Jeff Marshall, Lou Sabina, and Anisah Waite devoted time and effort to reviewing the literature, analyzing data, interviewing, and taking notes. Susan Gates and Laura Hamilton provided early assistance in conceptualizing the project and research design. Dan McCaffrey provided statistical consulting throughout the course of the project. Lynn Scott provided insightful feedback on our ideas and drafts.

The monograph itself was greatly improved through the efforts of reviewers and editors. Cathy Stasz served as a quality assurance reviewer and provided very useful feedback on document drafts. Rich Halverson and Paco Martorell served as peer reviewers. Both provided thoughtful and insightful reviews that led us to follow up on new leads in our data. Last, but certainly not least, Laura Zakaras's assistance in framing and drafting the messages was invaluable.

Abbreviations

APS	Atlanta Public Schools
AYP	adequate yearly progress
CCD	Common Core of Data
CCSSO	Council of Chief State School Officers
CLS	cohesive leadership system
CSSO	chief state school officer
DPAS II	Delaware Performance Appraisal System
ExEL	Executive Leadership Program for Educators
GLISI	Georgia Leadership Institute for School Improvement
IL-SAELP	Illinois State Action for Education Leadership Project
ISLLC	Interstate School Leaders Licensure Consortium
JCPS	Jefferson County Public Schools
NAEP	National Assessment of Educational Progress
NCES	National Center for Education Statistics
NCLB	No Child Left Behind
NISL	National Institute for School Leadership
OLN	Oregon Leadership Network
OLS	ordinary least squares
PD	professional development
RPDC	regional professional development center
SAELP	State Action for Education Leadership Project
SAM	school administration manager
SDD	SchoolDataDirect (an online service of the State Education Data Center)

SEA   state education agency
SREB   Southern Regional Education Board
SRT   school reform team
VAL-ED   Vanderbilt Assessment of Leadership in Education

CHAPTER ONE

Introduction

Researchers have identified school leadership as a key factor in improving schools and their students' achievement. In a recent review of the literature, Leithwood et al. (2004) concluded that among school-related factors that are associated with students' achievement, leadership is second only to classroom instruction. In addition, they found more demonstrated effects of successful leadership in low-performing schools. Although other factors, such as parental involvement, students' background, school characteristics, and the district context, should not be overlooked, certain practices on the part of principals have been found to be related to positive student outcomes, including increased student achievement (Waters, Marzano, and McNulty, 2003).

The research is less clear on what effective principals do to improve student achievement, as few empirical studies have examined this topic. The data that exist are mainly qualitative, making their generalizability questionable. At the same time, researchers are encouraged to take school context into greater consideration (Leithwood et al., 2004), arguing for research aimed less at the development of particular leadership models and more at discovering how flexibility is exercised by those in leadership roles.

These limitations notwithstanding, recent research suggests that effective principals spend more time in direct classroom supervision and support of teachers (NCSL, 2007), work with teachers to coordinate the school's instructional program, help solve instructional problems collaboratively, and help teachers secure resources and professional training (Heck, Larson, and Marcoulides, 1990). Principals may also improve student learning through their control of the curriculum and their power to select and motivate skilled teachers (Eberts and Stone, 1988; Brewer, 1993). As "instructional leaders," principals are expected to transform schools into learning-centered organizations by focusing them on student learning, creating communities of professionals in pursuit of that goal, and interfacing with external constituents to promote learning (CCSSO, 1996; Knapp, Copland, and Talbert, 2003).

Researchers and practitioners alike have described several problems that have systematically hindered cultivation of strong leaders. First, the education system has failed to attract high-quality candidates to the profession of school principal, particularly for schools that need them the most (Knapp, Copland, and Talbert, 2003). Part of the problem is that principals tend to self-select by enrolling in administrative certification programs. The literature suggests that the education system should do more to identify promising candidates and to entice them with better pay and conditions (Usdan, McCloud, and Podmostko, 2000; Norton et al., 2002; SREB, 2003, 2006; and Darling-Hammond et al., 2007).

Second, school leaders are not sufficiently prepared by pre-service programs, which have historically focused on managerial issues such as school law and administrative requirements and have failed to adequately address topics needed for instructional leadership such as instructional strategies, curriculum, and supporting teachers' professional growth (Copland, 1999; Elmore, 2000; Usdan, McCloud, and Podmostko, 2000). In addition, pre-service programs have typically not had strong clinical components that allow principals to gain practical knowledge and experience prior to leading their own schools (Peterson, 2002). There are many calls for the education system to hold pre-service programs accountable for strengthening student selection processes, improving the relevance and rigor of course content, and providing clinical experiences (Mazzeo, 2003; SREB, 2003, 2006; Davis et al., 2005; Darling-Hammond et al., 2007). In addition, policymakers have been encouraged to support alternative principal preparation programs (Mazzeo, 2003).

Third, the professional development (PD) offered to school leaders is considered weak and poorly connected to participants' needs (Coffin, 1997; Portin et al., 2003). Although the research on the impact of PD is not definitive, researchers argue that the education system needs to provide leaders with more sustained learning opportunities that are relevant to their career stage and linked to their needs (Peterson, 2002; Davis et al., 2005). This could include providing ongoing PD programs or institutes, as well as providing mentoring and/or coaching for new administrators (Usdan, McCloud, and Podmostko, 2000).

Fourth, the education system should establish rigorous leadership standards that reinforce expectations that principals will serve as instructional leaders (Usdan, McCloud, and Podmostko, 2000; Darling-Hammond et al., 2007). Such standards can be used to guide the updating of initial licensure and relicensure requirements. When linked to accreditation policies, standards can be used to hold preparation programs accountable for improving program content and structure. Standards can also motivate improvements in ongoing PD (Darling-Hammond et al., 2007).

Fifth, even when strong candidates are recruited and trained, the policy and programmatic environment often results in conditions that hinder them. Principals need supportive conditions such as access to data to inform their decisionmaking and authority to direct resources (people, time, and money). For example, effective leaders need autonomy to manage their own time as well as instructional and PD time for their staff (including setting calendars and daily schedules) (Portin et al., 2003).

In addition, effective leadership is enabled by personnel policies that not only allow leaders to make staffing decisions, but also provide efficient processes and support structures for recruiting, hiring, developing, and evaluating staff. Effective leadership is enabled by governance policies and structures that support organizational goals, clearly define roles and responsibilities of governing entities, assure role alignment and mutual accountability, and encourage stakeholder and parent engagement without interfering with autonomy (Portin et al., 2003; Vitaska, 2008).

Finally, the system within which principals work can either facilitate or obstruct effective leadership. The American education system has been described as fragmented, contradictory, and duplicative. Decisions are made in multiple arenas, at different levels of government, by many different actors. This leads to fragmentation among institutions both within and across government levels and inhibits the formation of coherent education policy (McDonnell, 2007).

In the late 1990s, The Wallace Foundation began to recognize the importance of school leadership and the lack of cohesion in education policies as an important issue. Since then, it has invested in a range of efforts to improve school leadership. These efforts have been aimed at involving multiple stakeholders in policymaking; basing programs, policies, and practices on high-quality leadership standards; and ensuring alignment across programs, policies, and practices. It is The Wallace Foundation's hypothesis that a more cohesive system supports improved school leadership, leading to improved teaching and learning.

The Cohesive Leadership System Hypothesis

By 2000, the emerging connection between strong instructional leaders and school improvement was making its way into state education policy discussions. The Interstate School Leaders Licensure Consortium (ISLLC) produced its first set of standards for school leaders in 1996 (CCSSO, 1996). At that time, some higher education institutions were beginning to rethink the conceptual cornerstones of their programs. The result was a shift from management theory to practices and behaviors of high-performing leaders and the standards they exemplify (Murphy, 2003). Several national and state-based policy organizations turned their attention to the recruitment, training, and retention of instructional leaders (see, e.g., Crews and Weakley, 1996; Murphy, Martin, and Muth, 1997; Hoyle, English, and Steffy, 1998). Pockets of research began to link school-leader behaviors to effective teaching and learning (e.g., Leithwood et al., 2004).

Within this context, The Wallace Foundation began its state initiative, the State Action for Education Leadership Project (SAELP) in 2000. Through SAELP, the Foundation provided funding to states to improve school leadership. A national consortium of state-based policy organizations was engaged in the management and support of the

SAELP initiative.[1] Its role was to support the initiative by helping state leaders forge an active state role to support developing a quality leader for every school (The Wallace Foundation, 2002). Shortly thereafter, Wallace decided to fund districts within its SAELP states.[2] It initially selected 17 districts and funded some at 20 times the level of the state funding. Funding will end for both states and districts on June 30, 2010.

In the early years of the state and district initiatives, Wallace program officers worked closely with their grantees, observing progress and noting obstacles across the sites. Foundation staff began to recognize the importance of the conditions that support leaders, such as resource allocation, decisionmaking and governance structures, incentives, and access to timely and adequate data. These conditions are influenced at both the state and the local levels, necessitating a two-way collaboration between states and districts to align state policies to district needs. Foundation staff concluded that creating better conditions for leaders required a systemwide, coordinated approach to developing policies aligned at state and district levels. They created informal, one-page system maps that depicted how states and districts were influencing each other. These maps reflected their emerging knowledge and a representation of what would later be hypothesized as the key elements of a cohesive leadership system (CLS) in the Foundation's publication *Leadership for Learning: Making the Connections Among State, District and School Policies and Practices* (The Wallace Foundation, 2006).

Figure 1.1 illustrates the Foundation's CLS hypothesis. The box on the left shows aligned actions undertaken by states and districts to set leadership standards and improve training and conditions for aspiring and current school leaders.

These actions support and enable effective leadership practices. Effective school leadership is evidenced by principals who have high expectations for students, use data to inform their decisions, and focus attention and resources on improving instruction. It is also achieved by school leadership teams that plan, implement, and evaluate improvements in instruction for all students. The outcome of interest—improved teaching and student achievement—is facilitated by effective school leadership.

This hypothesis raises three issues worth noting. First, it assumes that states and districts will be able to determine what principals should know and do to promote student achievement and that, once they make that determination, a cohesive system should be built around standards and expectations for school leaders. It is possible, however, that districts and states will not easily determine how to improve school leadership in ways that reliably improve student learning. Some critics argue that researchers have not yet found sufficient evidence that the leadership practices that are now pro-

---

[1] The partners included the Council of Chief State School Officers (CCSSO), the Education Commission of the States, the National Association of State Boards of Education, the National Conference of State Legislatures, and the National Governors Association.

[2] There were exceptions to this pattern. For example, Jefferson County Public Schools (JCPS) received funding from the Foundation before the state of Kentucky did.

Figure 1.1
The Wallace Foundation's Working Hypothesis of a CLS

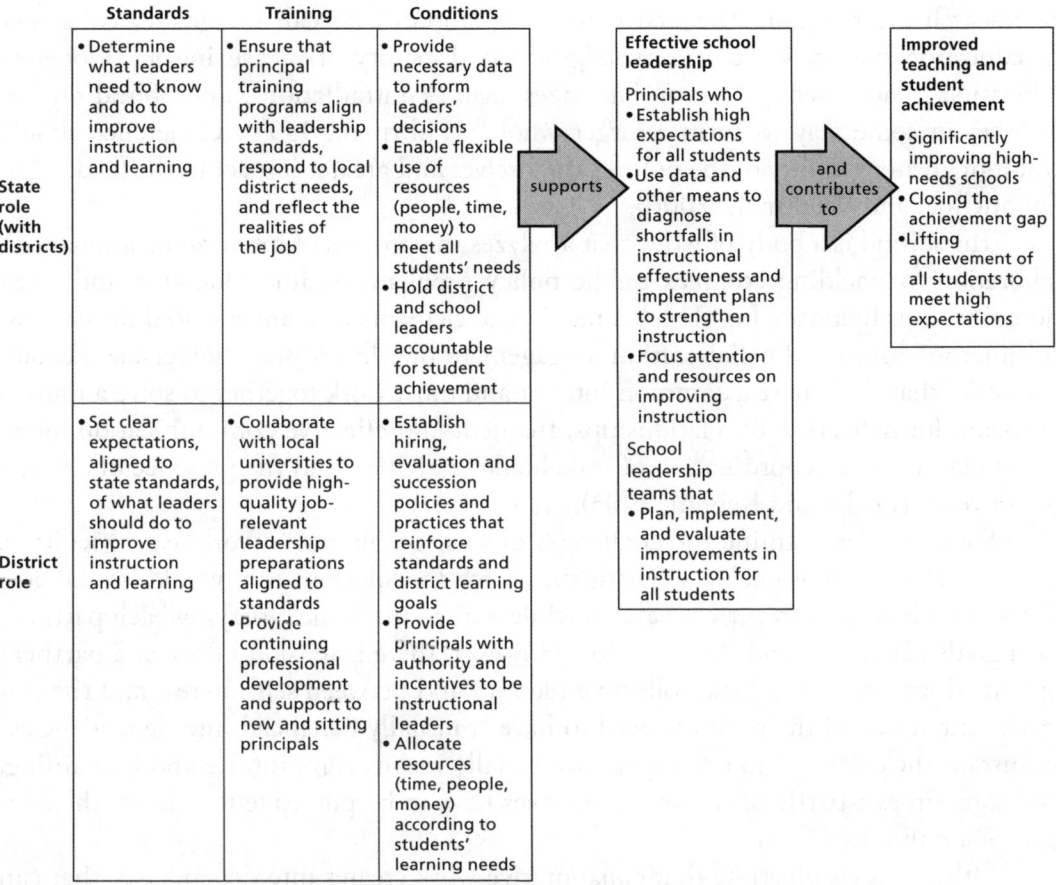

RAND *MG885-1.1*

moted will improve student learning. If that is the case, policymakers and practitioners have little empirical evidence to guide them, and cohesion could be built on unproven policies and initiatives. A set of policies may be coherent but not the appropriate solution to a problem (May, Sapotichne, and Workman, 2006). Second, the hypothesis does not focus on cohesion at the school level, although it could be argued that leadership teams would serve the function of aligning school-level practices and policies. Third, the hypothesis seems to ignore external risks to cohesion that could arise when other types of policies and initiatives interfere with or divert attention from leadership improvement initiatives. External threats to cohesion include, for example, teacher union contracts, lawsuits, community pressures, and local politics.

Research Relevant to Cohesive Leadership Systems

Although no existing studies analyze the Foundation's hypothesis directly, two bodies of research are relevant. The first consists of studies that call for greater coherence in education policy, while acknowledging the difficulty of measuring it. Coherent education policies send the same messages, avoid contradictions, and "build on one another in some way to form a larger whole" (Fuhrman, 1993). Coherence should result in greater stability of the policies themselves and greater impact in the field (May, Sapotichne, and Workman, 2006).

The second is a body of work that analyzes the process of interorganizational collaboration for tackling complex public policy problems within education and other domains. This literature highlights a number of elements that are essential for successful interorganizational collaboration: engagement of relevant stakeholders, stakeholders' belief that they share a common interest and must work together to solve a mutual problem, formalization of relationships, frequent and effective communication, organized planning and coordination of stakeholder activities, and the presence of a leader or convener (Legler and Reischl, 2003).

Some studies examine the challenges of such collaborative work (e.g., McGuire, 2006). Collaborations enable a synergistic search for solutions that would not be possible for each partner to perform alone, while at the same time satisfying each partner's own goals (Thomson and Perry, 2006). However, there is tension between a partner's own distinct identity and the collective identity and between self-interest and the collective interest, and the partners need to have "mutually beneficial interdependencies" to sustain the collaboration. Cooperation usually means compromise and bargaining, and sometimes a participant's own objectives have to be put aside to achieve the benefits of a mutual solution.

Other studies illustrate that collaborative work creates interdependency that can have either positive or negative consequences. Some argue that the process of cooperation among professional, public, and political actors results in long-term support and influence that transcends the particular issue that spurred the initial collaboration (Fuhrman, 1993). Although this long-term support can be beneficial, Bryson, Crosby, and Stone (2006) suggest that when systems become highly interconnected through cross-sector collaborations, changes in one sphere can reverberate unexpectedly through the system and there can be complex feedback loops with unintended consequences. Collaborations can also create new dependencies that complicate the policy environment, while each partner's control over that increasingly complex environment decreases (Thomson and Perry, 2006).

Because successful collaboration requires significant time and resources, some researchers have suggested that collaboration may be appropriate primarily for complex tasks (Thomson and Perry, 2006; Lundin, 2007). Building a CLS would be considered a complex task.

This literature provides cautious support for the Foundation's hypothesis. If states and districts are able to work together to build CLSs, they should be able to overcome policy fragmentation and improve consistency in policies and initiatives to improve leadership. They should carve out time and focus the attention of multiple stakeholders on improving school leadership, which the literature indicates is an important schooling component. Their joint work should also uncover promising practices at both the state and the district level, which would allow the state to better capitalize on and spread district successes. Ideally, if multiple partners are considering mechanisms to improve leadership, they will reference the most recent literature to the extent that it is useful but will also personalize efforts to their state context.

Objectives of This Study

The study reported here had three central objectives:

1. To document work undertaken in selected sites to build CLSs
2. To describe how such system-building is achieved and the strategies and contextual factors associated with the most advanced systems
3. To examine the CLS hypothesis that cohesion improves school leadership.

To meet the first objective, we synthesized existing literature to identify areas in which districts and states pursue policies and initiatives to improve school leadership: standards, pre-service/recruitment, licensure, evaluation, in-service, and principal conditions. We then analyzed activities in those policy areas in the sites.

We also analyzed the extent to which the policies and initiatives pursued in the sites formed a cohesive system. To do so, we reviewed the literature on system-building and developed a conceptual framework for assessing the presence of a CLS that included both structural and process dimensions. The structural dimensions of cohesive systems include comprehensiveness of leadership-related policies and initiatives and alignment of policies and practices within and between states and districts. The process dimensions include engagement of relevant stakeholders, agreement among stakeholders on the importance of school leadership and how it can be improved, and strong leadership that is capable of coordinating the work of multiple partners to build a CLS. We used these criteria to compare the extent to which cohesive systems had been achieved within the sites. By determining variance in the extent of cohesion built, we could better identify strategies and contextual characteristics that were associated with more-advanced CLSs.

Our second objective was to describe how the sites went about developing such systems and why there were variations in what sites had achieved. We analyzed the strategies the sites used and looked for differences between strategies used by sites that had achieved the most advanced systems and those used by the others. We also considered the contextual factors that enabled or hindered this work, such as a history of collaboration or strong preexisting social networks, staff turnover, and limited capacity within the state education agency (SEA).

Finally, we examined the hypothesis that a CLS improves school leadership. Because it was beyond the scope of the study to examine effects on student achievement—the ultimate goal of the CLS hypothesis—we focused on other potential effects. Specifically, we collected data from principals about their conditions and instructional leadership practices, two key components of the Wallace hypothesis. Attempts to survey principals about their training and about leadership standards proved less successful than questions about the conditions they faced and the instructional leadership practices they engaged in. Hence, we examined survey data from principals on their conditions, including the extent to which they reported having access to data, autonomy, and resources. Then we assessed whether principals who reported better conditions were more likely to be engaging in instructional leadership practices that are associated with improved student achievement, such as supporting the instruction of students. This approach was not sufficient to demonstrate that cohesion is a proven mechanism for improving school leadership and student achievement. Even showing a relationship between better conditions for principals and more time spent on instructional leadership is not sufficient to demonstrate that improved school leadership results in higher student achievement, since other factors may be influencing these outcomes. However, if we could demonstrate that principals reporting better conditions also spent more time on instructional leadership—and believed that the time was sufficient—this finding would offer some support for the Wallace hypothesis.

Organization of This Monograph

In Chapter Two, we describe the sites, data sources, and research methods used in the study. The rest of the monograph addresses the following research questions in this order:

1. **What policies and initiatives have states and districts pursued to improve school leadership?** Chapter Three describes the actions taken by both states and districts to improve school leadership.
2. **How are districts and states interacting to improve school leadership?** Chapter Four examines the different roles of states and districts as they worked together and separately to improve school leadership.
3. **To what extent have CLS sites built cohesion among policies and initiatives?** Using the indicators of cohesive systems we derived from the literature, we compare in Chapter Five the comprehensiveness of the policies and initia-

tives of the sites in our sample, the alignment among these policies and initiatives, and the collaborative efforts the sites used to build them. This enables us to distinguish the sites in terms of their relative success in establishing a CLS.

4. **How have sites built CLSs and why have some sites been more effective than others?** Chapter Six describes key strategies that sites have used to develop cohesion and identifies the inhibitors and facilitators of those strategies. We then determine whether the more cohesive sites vary along these dimensions.

5. **How are sites attempting to scale up and sustain their work?** In Chapter Seven, we explore efforts to scale up and sustain the progress made to date, noting challenges to sustainment and expansion and strategies for sustainment and growth.

6. **Do we find support for the CLS hypothesis?** In Chapter Eight, we examine whether principals who report positive conditions also spend more time on practices that relate to quality of instruction and whether they reported that this time spent was sufficient to meet the needs of their schools.

7. **What are the policy implications of our findings?** In Chapter Nine, we draw lessons from our analysis for other states and districts that are trying to build closer working relationships and more aligned systems in support of educational reform.

Caveats

This study had several limitations, some of which are important to the interpretation of our results. First, as we have mentioned, we were not able to analyze the effects of more-cohesive systems on student achievement. Nor can we make causal claims about the relationship between the cohesiveness of policies within a site and effective leadership practices. We did not survey principals over time to see whether they noted differences in conditions or their ability to focus on instructional leadership as cohesion developed between their district and state.

Second, although we recognize that the term *school leadership* encompasses a broad array of leaders, we focused mainly on principals. Although we asked district and state interviewees about efforts to improve leadership for aspiring leaders and supporting actors, such as school board members, we did not systematically interview or survey teachers, school leaders other than principals, or school board members.

Third, we did not measure the relative effectiveness of particular leadership policies and practices implemented by each site. We looked at the comprehensiveness of these actions, but not at their effectiveness: In other words, we cannot say whether the actions we document are likely to lead to improvements in school leadership.

Fourth, we did not examine cohesion within individual schools. Some of the literature we examined (e.g., Newmann et al., 2001) discusses within-school instructional program coherence. However, this was not a topic of our research, given that the Wallace model does not address this level of cohesion. Nor did we examine cohesion within particular districts. Although we examined actions districts were taking to improve school leadership in an aligned fashion, we reserved the term *cohesive* to refer to the relationship between the state and its affiliated districts, to reflect the full CLS hypothesis.

Fifth, since the selected sites were working to improve school leadership through funding from The Wallace Foundation, they represent exemplars and not more typical examples of what we might find in other locations throughout the country.

Finally, we were not able to generalize our findings across an entire state. We focused on the work being done at the state level in conjunction with one to three districts in each state. Although much of the work done at the state level had the potential to affect all districts in a state, our data collection and analysis were limited to the relationship between state organizations and selected affiliate districts.

Despite these limitations, however, this study provides an extensive analysis of what can be done when states and districts commit themselves to working together toward the common goal of improving school leadership.

CHAPTER TWO

Data Sources and Analytic Approach

To answer the study questions, we employed a cross-site comparative case-study design and both qualitative and quantitative research methods. We used multiple sources of data to triangulate findings within and across sites. We analyzed data from documents, interviews, principal surveys, and principal end-of-day logs, noting both confirming and refuting evidence. This chapter describes site selection, data sources, and our cross-site analytic approach.

Study Site Selection

In 2007, The Wallace Foundation took stock of progress in 21 states and several more districts that it had been funding and otherwise supporting and classified them into one of three categories: CLS, aligned system of leader development, or leadership network. Sites in the *CLS* category were those making the most progress toward connecting state and district policies affecting leadership standards and training; they were making progress on improving at least three different conditions for school leaders that should positively impact instructional leadership and lead to improved teaching and learning. Those in the *aligned system of leader development* category were making progress on creating aligned policies and initiatives focused primarily on training. These sites were addressing only one condition. Sites in the *leadership network* category were deemed to be making less progress on creating aligned systems. These categories have dictated funding and support levels from the Foundation for the past two years.

The Foundation and our study team purposively selected 10 of the 21 funded state/district sites representing a range of progress in developing a CLS. Table 2.1 lists the selected sites and the Wallace classification of each state and district. Each site consists of one state plus one to three affiliated districts. Although each state and each district pursued some initiatives independently, our study focused on the CLSs being built by the states and their partner districts.

Table 2.1
Sites Selected for the Study by Wallace Classification

State and School Districts	Wallace Category
Delaware	CLS
Appoquinimink	—
Christina	—
Indian River	—
Georgia	CLS
Atlanta	CLS
Illinois	CLS
Chicago	CLS
Springfield	CLS
Indiana	Network
Fort Wayne	Aligned
Iowa	CLS
Clear Creek Amana	—
Davenport	—
Waterloo	—
Kentucky	CLS
Jefferson County	CLS
Massachusetts	CLS
Boston	CLS
Springfield	CLS
Missouri	Aligned
St. Louis	Aligned
Oregon	Aligned
Eugene	Aligned
Portland	Aligned
Rhode Island	Network
Providence	Aligned

Table 2.2 lists the funding levels and duration of funding for the selected sites. The organizations listed in italics are the grantees of record for the state funding. The districts in boldface are those that received direct funding from the Foundation. Only districts in Delaware and Iowa did not receive direct funding; the Foundation grants made to these states were used to influence multiple districts. Funding varied from $6.1 million in Iowa to $13.8 million in Massachusetts. Funding to Boston, Chicago, and Portland school districts started in 2005, and in Kentucky, JCPS was funded before the state received funding.

The sites differed in some fundamental ways, which we considered in our analyses of the data. First, they differed in the number of districts studied. Second, as noted in the tables, not all districts were Wallace grantees—those without any CLS category designation in Table 2.1 did not receive direct funding from the Foundation. Third, two districts—Providence and Fort Wayne—were categorized differently from their states. The Foundation deemed that these two districts were making more progress than their states in improving school leadership.

Table 2.2
Wallace Education Leadership Grants for Study Sites (projected through June 2010)

Site	Years of Funding	Approximate Total Funding ($ millions)
Delaware and partner districts (*DE Department of Education*) Appoquinimink Christina Indian River	2001–2010	6.5
Georgia and partner districts (*University System of GA Fdn Inc.*)	2001–2010	5.6
Atlanta Public Schools	2001–2010	6.2
Illinois and partner districts (*IL State University*)	2001–2010	5.3
Chicago Public Schools	2005–2010	3.2
Springfield School District 186	2001–2010	5.0
Indiana and partner districts (*IN Department of Education*)	2001–2010	1.3
Fort Wayne Community Schools	2001–2010	7.7
Iowa and partner districts (*IA Department of Education*) Clear Creek Amana Davenport Waterloo	2001–2010	6.1
Kentucky and partner districts (*KY Department of Education*)	2003–2010	3.1
Jefferson County Public Schools	2001–2010	8.7
Massachusetts and partner districts (*MA Department of Education*)	2001–2010	2.9
Boston Public Schools	2005–2010	2.9
Springfield Public Schools	2001–2010	8.0
Missouri and partner districts (*MO Department of Elementary & Secondary Education*)	2001–2010	2.7
St. Louis Public Schools	2001–2010	5.0
Oregon and partner districts (*OR Department of Education*)	2001–2010	4.1
Eugene School District 4J	2001–2010	5.6
Portland Public Schools	2005–2010	0.9
Rhode Island and partner districts (*RI State Department of Elementary & Secondary Education*)	2001–2010	1.4
Providence School Department	2001–2010	7.0
Total	—	99.2

The study sites also varied greatly with respect to region, enrollment, percentage of minority students, progress in academic achievement, and, for districts, urbanicity. Details of the sociodemographic characteristics and trends in academic achievement of the sites are given in Appendix A.

Data Sources

From February through November 2008, we systematically gathered information across all the selected sites on the policies and initiatives they were developing and implementing to improve school leadership and the strategies they had enacted to develop cohesion. At the start of the project, we interviewed 10 experts in school leadership to inform the development of our analytic framework and the interview and survey instruments. We collected most of our other data from interviews with representatives of district, state, and pre-service principal preparation programs, and we supplemented that information with a review of websites and progress reports and other project documents sent to the Foundation. To assess principals' conditions and time spent on instructional leadership practices, we interviewed, surveyed, and captured log data from principals in the 17 study districts. We describe each data collection effort below.

Interviews

Interviews with state officials, district representatives, and principal preparation and development providers focused on the leadership improvement initiatives under way in each state and district, as well as the nature of the development of CLSs. Our protocols were designed to gather data on the following topics:

- Knowledge of the Foundation's work in education leadership
- Key policies and initiatives pursued to improve school leadership as they related to standards, pre-service preparation, licensure, evaluation processes, in-service PD, and conditions
- Initiative-specific strategies, alignment efforts, satisfaction level, enablers and hindrances, and sustainability
- Cohesion with respect to coordination, breadth of engagement, common vision, alignment, improvement efforts, and factors that enable or hinder cohesion
- The impact of these initiatives
- State and district constraints, competition with other student achievement improvement efforts, and unexpected negative consequences
- Recommendations for improving school leadership and building cohesion.

Further questions depended on the role of the individual interviewee in specific initiatives. Interviews lasted 60 to 90 minutes.

We used a set of indicators to guide the design of the interview protocols and analysis codes (see Appendix B for a complete list of these indicators). We used the indicator lists to question respondents about different types of actions that the literature suggests states and districts should be taking, such as providing internships as part of pre-service training; elements or strategies for cohesion; and supports or conditions for principals.

In each state, we interviewed members of organizations involved in the development or implementation of leadership improvement policies and initiatives, including staff of SEAs; state boards of primary, secondary, and higher education; and representatives of principals' associations and teachers' unions. In each district, we interviewed district leaders and administrators associated with principal selection, supervision, and support, as well as administrators overseeing curriculum and other academic operations.

State and district interviewees were identified in two ways. First, site visit teams conducted telephone interviews with the grantee of record (the organization receiving Wallace funding), if relevant, in each state and district. Grantees of record at the state level included SEAs, university centers, and professional associations. In districts, the grantee of record was typically the district central office. We asked members at each grantee of record to suggest interviewees in the state and district(s) who were involved in leadership development efforts.

We also interviewed a representative from the governor's office and/or from the legislature in each state, so that we did not have to rely solely on recommendations from Wallace grantees and to get a sense of how efforts to promote the development of school leaders across the state or within a district corresponded with broader efforts to improve student achievement. Similarly, in 15 of the 17 districts, we were able to interview someone from the superintendent's office and someone who oversees curriculum and instruction.

To capture principals' perspectives on the conditions that enable or hinder their leadership, site visit teams interviewed four to 10 principals in each district at the primary school, middle school, and high school levels. Our interviewees were district-defined "high-performing" principals. Although we initially asked districts to schedule interviews with a random selection of principals, we discovered in our first site visit that district contacts set up interviews with principals that they deem high-performing. We therefore decided to integrate this propensity into our research design. It is important to note that the selection of high-performing principals could lead to selection bias issues in our interview data, in that principals deemed to be lower-performing might perceive challenges to their job as well as conditions as different in nature and degree from those of higher-performing principals. Although we were unable to capture that information in the interviews, we assumed that the conditions highlighted by high-performing principals as hindering their work were likely obstacles to lower-performing principals as well.

The principal-interview protocol elicited detailed information on conditions at the school, district, and state levels and how those conditions enabled or hindered the principals' ability to improve or ensure student learning in their schools. Questions covered the following topics:

- The principal's background and training experiences and their relevancy to his or her current role
- Experience with state and district programs or policies to improve school leadership as they relate to standards, pre-service preparation, licensure, evaluation processes, in-service PD, and conditions
- The degree to which the initiatives support leadership development and practice, whether they are aligned to state leadership standards, and whether they address the most critical issues facing the principal or his or her school
- Identification of critical leadership strategies and actions undertaken and which of them the principal prioritized
- Facilitators of and barriers to effective leadership, including (but not limited to) autonomy, sufficient support (with respect to data, curriculum, professional staff, recruitment and dismissal of teachers, and building parental and community engagement), allocation of resources, relationships with the local school council/ board of education and teachers' union, and school culture
- Recommendations for the state or district that might enable more effective school leadership.

The site visit teams conducted a total of 396 interviews. Table 2.3 shows the number of interviewees in each state. Numbers of interviewees varied according to the number of people and organizations involved in a site's leadership improvement efforts.

Survey

The survey enabled us to explore principals' conditions and time spent on leadership practices across all the districts in our study. The surveys were administered online to

Table 2.3
Total Number of Interviews by State and Role

State	State Officials	District Officials[a]	Principals	Training Providers	Total
Delaware	20	18 (3)	11	7	56
Georgia	9	13 (1)	4	1	27
Illinois	12	13 (2)	11	6	42
Indiana	7	8 (1)	7	6	28
Iowa	26	18 (3)	14	6	64
Kentucky	8	8 (1)	6	16	38
Massachusetts	13	15 (2)	11	1	40
Missouri	8	8 (1)	5	9	30
Oregon	11	14 (2)	19	3	47
Rhode Island	7	10 (1)	4	3	24
Total	121	125	92	58	396

[a]Numbers in parentheses indicate the number of districts in the study.

all the principals in our study districts between late May and mid-June 2008, corresponding with the end of the academic year of each district; follow-up efforts continued through September 2008. The survey instrument drew on the Foundation's CLS framework, literature on effective leadership practices, 1996 ISLLC standards,[1] and measures validated in other studies on leadership practices.[2] We asked principals to reflect on the 2007–2008 academic year when answering questions on district- and state-level support; conditions; time spent, and the appropriateness of the time spent, on a range of leadership practices; school culture and climate; and the amount and type of pre-service training the principal received prior to becoming a principal. We pilot-tested the survey with six principals and made adjustments based on those results.

We received a 40 percent response rate (624 out of 1,582). To adjust for potential differences due to nonresponse, we created weights that reflected response probabilities at the school level so that our responding sample would be representative of the entire population of principals in each district.[3] We used these weighted data in our survey analyses. We did not replace or impute missing data. A description of the administration of the survey, response rates by district, characteristics of the schools (including student performance), and weighting methodology is given in Appendix C.

End-of-Day Logs

To gather more-detailed information on how specific conditions helped or hindered principals in their daily activities, we asked approximately 10 principals in each district (a total of 167 principals) to complete an end-of-day log at the end of each workday for one week in October 2008 and one week in November 2008; the logs were completed via the Internet. As we did for the principal interviews, we asked districts to supply us with names of effective principals. The log form asked principals to reflect on their working day and to report on the conditions that supported or hindered them from performing instructional leadership practices during that day. Appendix D presents details on the end-of-day log development and analysis.

Table 2.4 summarizes the primary data sources used to address our first six research questions.

---

[1] The 2008 ISLLC standards were not available at the time the survey was developed. However, we performed a validity check to ensure that the 2008 ISLLC professional standards were covered in our survey.

[2] We used questions from a survey developed for a RAND study on new leaders for new schools (publication in progress).

[3] Responding principals were more likely to work in schools that had significantly higher reading and mathematics test scores and lower percentages of minority students and students receiving free or reduced lunches than the schools of nonresponding principals. The differences between responding and nonresponding principals were accommodated through our weighting methodology, as explained in Appendix C.

Table 2.4
Research Questions and Primary Data Sources

Research Question	Data Source
1. What policies and initiatives have states and districts pursued to improve school leadership?	• State interviews • District interviews
2. How are districts and states interacting to improve school leadership?	• State interviews • District interviews
3. To what extent have sites built cohesion among these policies and initiatives?	• State interviews • District interviews
4. How have sites built CLSs and why have some sites been more effective than others?	• State interviews • District interviews
5. How are sites attempting to scale up and sustain their work?	• State interviews • District interviews
6. Do we find support for the CLS hypothesis?	• Principal surveys • Principal end-of-day logs • Principal interviews

Analytic Approach

What Policies and Initiatives Have States and Districts Pursued to Improve School Leadership?

To answer this first research question, we analyzed data from the interview notes in a multistep process. When researchers returned from the field, they compiled their notes in summaries with separate thematic areas (e.g., "state policies and initiatives" and "strategies for building cohesion"). They wrote one summary for each state and separate summaries for each district. The summaries were reviewed by all team members and discussed in a debriefing meeting for each site. The thematic areas were each compiled into Atlas.ti[4] as separate reports. For example, one report detailed all 10 sites' policies and initiatives. Another report focused on strategies for building cohesion. These reports were analyzed and summarized into tables which each site leader checked for accuracy. For additional verification, a representative from each of the 27 study states and districts was invited to review a draft version of this report for comment. Throughout our analyses, we tracked multiple stakeholder perspectives and examined refuting evidence, placing notes in the text identifying any point on which there were divergent views.

How Are Districts and States Interacting to Improve School Leadership?

We analyzed the site summaries to identify patterns across the 10 study sites on whether the district or the state was taking the lead role in improving student achievement. We

---

[4] Software for qualitative analysis of large bodies of data.

also examined how districts and states were learning from each other to improve their initiatives. Finally, we analyzed the site summaries to identify individuals and organizations taking lead roles at the district and state levels.

To What Extent Have CLS Sites Built Cohesion Among Policies and Initiatives?

We analyzed the site summaries to ascertain the extent to which sites were building a CLS by mapping efforts for only the six sites determined by the Foundation to be making progress toward the goal of building a CLS. On the basis of the Wallace model and the broader literature, we identified five dimensions of cohesion:

- *Comprehensiveness* of the six leadership policy areas that made up the core efforts of states and districts to improve school leadership (i.e., standards, pre-service and recruitment, licensure, evaluation, in-service, and improving conditions)
- *Alignment* of policies and practices within and between levels of the system (state and district)
- *Engagement* of relevant stakeholders in the development and implementation of the CLS
- *Agreement* among stakeholders regarding how to improve school leadership.
- *Coordination* that promotes alignment, engagement, and agreement around leadership development initiatives.

To address the first dimension, comprehensiveness, we analyzed the extent to which sites had developed policies and initiatives across the six policy areas. The sites designated as more comprehensive were implementing more policies and initiatives and/or were focused on the continuum of leadership (from ensuring a steady pipeline of principals to principal retirement) and the breadth of school leaders (ranging from leaders within schools, such as teacher leaders or administrative staff, through higher-level district or state school leaders, such as school board members). For example, while two sites may have taken concrete actions to improve pre-service education, a site that employed a combination of approaches to spur redesign of all preparation programs in the state would be rated higher on comprehensiveness than a site that relied on school district partnerships alone to try to influence local pre-service programs.

We next looked for evidence of policies, programs, and approaches that promoted alignment among components of the system and between state and district practices. We looked for evidence of alignment across initiatives and levels (or no significant evidence of misalignment). Sites designated as building a CLS through engagement, agreement, and coordination met the following criteria: consistent reports that most relevant stakeholders were involved in initiative design and/or implementation; consistent reports that there was broad agreement on the importance of leadership and on the approaches to improving it (including consensus reached after earlier disagreement); and evidence that an organization and/or individual actively coordinated across initiatives and between state and district programs and practices. Throughout our analysis, we again noted patterns of discord, as well as disconfirming evidence.

How Have Sites Built CLSs and Why Have Some Sites Been More Effective Than Others?

To better understand how states and districts built CLSs, we analyzed the state and district interview data that described strategies for building cohesion and contextual factors enabling or hindering states' work in this regard. To determine patterns, we compared the more advanced CLS sites against all the other sites.

How Are Sites Attempting to Scale Up and Sustain Their Work?

We used state and district interview data to document how sites were attempting to scale up and sustain their work. To answer the question, we mapped the challenges and sustainment strategies reported by interviewees.

Do We Find Support for the CLS Hypothesis?

Our ability to answer this question was limited. We focused on the relationship between favorable conditions facing principals (e.g., access to data, sufficient resources) and the time they spent on instructional leadership (and how satisfied they were with this allocation of time). To understand whether favorable conditions were positively related to instructional leadership practices, as posited by the CLS hypothesis, we analyzed the responses on the principal surveys to questions about conditions encountered in their daily work lives and the amount of time spent on specific instructional leadership practices over the course of the 2007–2008 academic year. We focused on key conditions drawn from the literature and the Wallace model, and we created four indices based on our data: the nature of state and district data; adequacy of resources; level of autonomy; and the nature of district-provided evaluations, PD, and other tools. We analyzed responses on four survey questions to measure the remaining conditions: alignment of governance roles and responsibilities; fragmentation, misalignment, or burden of policies; quality of administrative staff in the school; and district provision of administrative support to the principal.

We also created nine indices of instructional leadership practices, organized around three broad categories: the development and implementation of strategic goals and school improvement efforts; supporting the instruction of students; and promoting the development and leadership of the school's teachers and staff. These indices were based on recent studies researching the leadership practices that are most effective in supporting instruction and student learning in schools and on Wallace's CLS hypothesis. Details on the survey questions used to create the indices and the construction of the indices are given in Appendix E.

To better isolate whether there is a relationship between conditions and instructional leadership practices, we conducted regression analyses that controlled for reading proficiency levels of the students in the school, the percentage of economically dis-advantaged students, total student enrollment, the percentage of African-Americans in the student body, and the grade level of the school. We included the principal's district in each analysis and controlled for the principal's years of experience in the school. Results of the regression analyses are given in Appendix F. Finally, to illustrate the relationship between conditions and principals' reported leadership practices, we provide some sample responses from the interviews and from the open-ended questions on the surveys and logs in the discussion in Chapter Eight.

CHAPTER THREE

Policies and Initiatives Taken to Improve Leadership

The Wallace Foundation's CLS hypothesis asserts that districts and states should take actions to support leadership improvement in three key policy areas: standards, training, and conditions and incentives (The Wallace Foundation, 2006). Based on the literature and our early examination of the study sites, we expanded this grouping to six policy areas: standards, pre-service and recruitment, licensure, evaluation, in-service, and conditions. We examined the 10 states and 17 districts separately to detail the types of policies and initiatives implemented at both levels, then we drew some comparisons among them. As expected, there was a good deal of variation across sites. Some sites, for example, pursued multiple initiatives; others focused on just a few. Some sites pursued an aggressive strategy of reform; others chose a more limited approach.

We did not try to evaluate progress on the basis of the number and type of policies and initiatives the sites were pursuing. For example, it is likely that some sites that focused on fewer actions may have been implementing them in ways that affect a greater number of school leaders. We also did not try to measure the quality or impact of particular initiatives but focused instead on describing them in all their diversity.

Types of Policies and Initiatives

Standards

States and districts in our study tended to pursue the following initiatives with regard to leadership standards: setting statewide standards, updating standards, and broadening the positions addressed by standards.

Setting statewide standards. All 10 states had statewide leadership standards that were aligned with national standards. Some states, including Delaware and Rhode Island, simply adopted the ISLLC standards. Most others created their own standards based on the ISLLC standards. (One exception was Oregon, which based its standards on the national Educational Leadership Constituent Council standards.) Some states engaged in an iterative process to gather input from various stakeholders to create standards. For example, the School Administrators of Iowa used funding from the Foundation to convene a group of approximately 95 superintendents in September 2006 to review draft standards and criteria in light of recent Mid-Continent Research for Education and Learning findings on superintendent behaviors that are correlated with high student achievement. A second group of about 35 principals and superintendents met in October 2006 to continue the process and to finalize agreed-upon standards and criteria.

Although all states had statewide standards, five of the 17 districts we studied chose to draft their own district-level standards or competencies. Most of these standards were based on the state standards but provided further district-specific elaboration.

Updating standards. Most of the states that based their statewide leadership standards on the ISLLC standards had updated or were in the process of updating them to align with the new 2008 ISLLC standards.

Three districts were providing significant input into the revision of the state-level standards. According to both state and district respondents, Jefferson County's district-level work in adding specifications to standards was highly influential in initiating the statewide revision effort. In Massachusetts, two representatives from Boston and three from Springfield were key members of a state-level team charged with revising the state standards.

Broadening positions addressed by standards. Five of the 10 states were broadening the positions addressed by leadership standards. Three states were attempting to specify standards for master principals or others who mentor or coach principals. The standards sent to the Rhode Island Board of Regents in November 2008 for approval covered a continuum of school leaders, including principals, central office administrators, building administrators, teacher leaders, department chairs, and any educator with leadership responsibilities. No districts reported broadening positions addressed by standards (although Boston and Springfield were assisting the state in thinking about how to do this).

Pre-Service and Recruitment

Many states and districts were reforming their pre-service programs to better align them with their standards for leadership and districts' needs. States and districts tended to pursue the following types of pre-service and recruitment policies and initiatives: sunsetting accreditation for pre-service programs and requiring programs to reapply for accreditation; collaboratively redesigning pre-service programs; creating alternative preparation programs; offering training and experiences aimed at increasing interest and knowledge about the principal position; and improving recruitment efforts.

Sunset policies. Some states, including Georgia and Iowa, sunset all pre-service leadership programs, thereby forcing them to reapply for accreditation. The Iowa Department of Education and State Board of Education jointly decided to sunset all leadership programs in 2004 after a task force determined that the programs were not producing high-quality leaders. States taking this action viewed it as necessary, because they had found that without this type of accountability, universities were reluctant to reform their programs. Some interviewees said that universities did not have incentives to improve the rigor of their programs because it might discourage candidates from enrolling and completing them, thereby decreasing revenue. Others reported that individual professors who were used to autonomy in designing programs did not have incentives to revise their structure and content. Sunsetting policies was intended to address both types of concerns by providing the incentive for change.

Collaborative redesign of programs. Another way in which districts and states attempted to improve pre-service programs was through collaborative efforts to re-design them. In Oregon, representatives from eight pre-service programs decided to work together, and in 2003 they formed a nonprofit group called the Oregon Professors of Educational Administration to craft new standards for their programs. The group is a state affiliate of the National Council of Professors of Educational Administration. At the district level, Jefferson County collaborated with the University of Louisville to redesign its principal preparation program to be more aligned with dimensions of effective leadership espoused by the Southern Regional Education Board (SREB), The Wallace Foundation, and ISLLC. This redesign effort was later expanded statewide.

Alternative preparation programs. Both districts and states were attempt-ing to improve pre-service and recruitment by creating new preparation programs. These programs sometimes replaced traditional pre-service programs, and many were designed to meet specific district needs. For example, since 2003, Boston has operated a "grow-your-own" principal preparation program called the Boston Principal Fellow-ship program. The program includes 90 days of coursework and full-year residency with a Boston principal four days per week. Participants commit to three years with the Boston Public Schools after completion of the program. The curriculum is taught by school system staff, higher education faculty, and community leaders and targets knowledge the participants need to be a principal in the Boston school system. Several other district-based alternative programs similarly include targeted recruiting, district-specific curriculum, and residency components. Some of these programs gained the ability to license their graduates, and some became a much more common pathway to becoming a principal than local university-based preparation programs.

Increasing interest in and knowledge about the principal position. At least three districts offered pre-service PD programs for teacher and school leaders (other than principals) to expose them to and prepare them for leadership opportunities. For example, the Instructional Leadership Institute in Boston is a non-licensure program for school-based administrators and teacher leaders designed to develop their leader-ship potential and skills. In Springfield, MA, teachers can apply to be either "instruc-tional leadership specialists" or "teacher leaders," to serve as demonstrators, co-teachers, and coach/mentors. These programs typically aim not only to build current leadership skills that can be applied in school and teacher leader roles, but also to generate interest in pursuing a principal position.

Interviewees described other programs that were more explicitly aimed at building interest in becoming a principal. These programs provided PD for school leaders (such as teacher leaders and coaches) that served as an introduction to the principal position, and some provided opportunities for participants to shadow principals. For example, Fort Wayne offered an investigative series that provided opportunities for individuals with an interest in an administrative career to meet with current school leaders to explore "just what principals do." The investigative series involved voluntary quarterly after-school meetings and one day of release time to shadow a principal.

Targeted recruitment and succession-planning efforts. Another action taken by districts—often in conjunction with some of the pre-service programs described above—was targeting recruitment of particular individuals or programs. This approach was utilized by just over half of the districts we studied. In some cases, it involved recruiting graduates from particular pre-service programs. For example, many districts gave hiring preference to individuals who had participated in the district-based pre-service program. The instructors in many of these programs were district personnel who were familiar with the students and were able to target recruitment efforts toward the strongest ones.

In other cases, particular teachers or school leaders within the district who had demonstrated leadership potential were identified and encouraged to enter a pre-service program. Appoquinimink carefully selected promising leaders from among its teachers and encouraged them to apply for the Appoquinimink Aspiring Administrators program.

Across these different types of pre-service policies and initiatives, districts and states incentivized programs to be more selective, provided more context-specific curriculum, included internships, and addressed new research-based notions of what leaders need to know and be able to do, such as engage in instructional leadership and develop cultural competencies.

Licensure

Changing licensure policies was another approach highlighted by the literature and our respondents for both improving the quality of school leaders and providing alternative pathways to leadership positions. We found that these policy changes were pursued exclusively by states. In Massachusetts, the Boston and Springfield districts, however, were also granted the ability to license graduates of their own district-based preparation programs. Some states had changed or attempted to change their licensing structure. For example, Indiana eliminated the elementary and secondary school distinction; Rhode Island tried to remove grade-level distinctions, but it failed. Oregon reduced the number of levels of administrative licenses from three to two and increased the experience requirements for the second level. Similarly, at least four other states created a continuum of licenses to specify at least two, and sometimes three, levels for the principal license. Delaware instituted a three-tier system that provided initial, continuing, and advanced licenses. Rhode Island provided a school leader license, Kentucky provided a teacher leader endorsement, and Illinois provided a teacher leader license and a master principal license.

Some states reformed their licensure systems by revising the requirements for initial licensure and relicensure. Indiana, Iowa, and Oregon revised their requirements to align with the new ISLLC leadership standards. At the time of our data collection, the Georgia legislature was considering performance-based requirements for relicensure, and Massachusetts was considering revising licensure requirements to align with newly drafted standards.

Finally, some states created alternative licensure routes. Illinois created an alternative route to an administrator license for National Board Certified teachers, and Delaware created an alternative route for teacher leaders. As mentioned above, Massachusetts granted approval for the alternative licensure routes created by the Boston and Springfield school districts. These routes were created to increase competition among traditional preparation programs and also to provide additional routes to becoming a principal, reducing barriers to this role.

Evaluation

During the time of our study, many study states and districts were pursuing policies and initiatives for evaluating leaders. Although the CLS hypothesis emphasizes evaluation as an important condition, respondents also highlighted it as an important policy lever they could use to directly improve leadership. Georgia, Illinois, Kentucky, and Iowa were requiring that all principals in the state be evaluated, but they did not require a specific approach (although they did supply models and guidelines to assist in this process). This was noteworthy given that principals are often evaluated infrequently or not at all (Usdan, McCloud, and Podmostko, 2000). Some states and districts were creating or implementing a common evaluation system. For example, Delaware developed the Delaware Performance Appraisal System (DPAS II) for administrators, which is designed to measure progress according to the ISLLC standards. To rate principals, evaluators review evidence submitted by the principal; outcomes of three conferences (goal setting, formative, and summative) between the principal and the evaluator; survey data from principals, teachers, and evaluators; and student achievement and growth data from state and local assessments. This evaluation system was being used by the three districts we visited in Delaware.

Some states and districts were either creating or making available an evaluation tool. Several sites, including Jefferson County, were piloting the Vanderbilt Assessment of Leadership in Education (VAL-ED) leadership assessment tool. Funded by The Wallace Foundation and created by Vanderbilt University, VAL-ED utilizes a multirater, evidence-based approach to assess school leadership behaviors that research has demonstrated influence teacher performance and student learning.

In the process of revising evaluation processes and tools, several states and districts were shifting the focus of evaluation to be more supportive of professional growth. For example, new administrators in Iowa must be evaluated at least once every three years to ensure continuous improvement. The evaluation process is intended to support growth toward goals outlined in individual professional growth plans.

In-Service Professional Development

Both states and districts provided PD for practicing leaders, including programs, mentors, coaches, and networks to support professional growth.

PD programs. Almost every state and district provided some kind of PD program; several were cohort-based, i.e., a group of individuals—such as school-based or district-based teams—went through a program together. Massachusetts made a national instructional leadership program, the National Institute for School Leadership (NISL), available to all principals in the state. This intensive program required participants to attend two days of training every month for a year and a half. The program primarily targeted principals, but districts were encouraged to attend as leadership teams that included central office staff. Several states and their affiliated districts also participated in one of two national programs sponsored by The Wallace Foundation. The Executive Leadership Program for Educators at the University of Virginia is a collaborative effort of The Darden Graduate School of Business Administration and the Curry School of Education. Harvard University's Executive Leadership Program for Educators (ExEL) is also a collaborative effort, offered through the Harvard Business School, the Harvard Graduate School of Education, and the John F. Kennedy School of Government. Both programs have recruited teams of state, district, and school leaders to focus on pressing problems facing education leaders. The programs are explicitly trying to improve the ways in which states and districts work together to address these challenges.

Mentors. Almost all study states emphasized mentoring for new principals for their first year or two. Several states required districts to provide mentors to new principals. Others administered the mentor program, and districts enrolled their principals in it. In Iowa, districts were able to provide their own programs, but most opted into the statewide program. At least three states also provided mentoring to several different types of school leaders, including superintendents, district office staff, and assistant principals.

Coaches. Some states and districts provided coaches, in addition to mentors. Coaches often provide more-intensive guidance regarding how to operationalize ideas from PD programs. For example, Massachusetts provided coaches to support principals and superintendents in implementing ideas from the NISL training it provided to all districts and principals.

Networks. Some states and districts attempted to support professional learning by organizing networks of school and/or district leaders to support each other's learning, often as part of a professional learning community. Leaders in Kentucky scaled a program developed by Jefferson County Public Schools, the Kentucky Instructional Leadership Team Network. This network supported schools and districts in the development and operation of instructional leadership teams that operated as "professional learning communities." These learning communities supported principals, as members of school-based teams, in learning about instructional strategies and interventions. Massachusetts organized its own Urban Superintendents' Network, which has reportedly functioned as a professional learning community to study and address challenges faced by urban districts in the state.

Improving Conditions

The CLS hypothesis asserts that if states and districts collaborate on policies and practices that improve conditions for principals, these conditions will support principals' ability to enact effective leadership practices. Conditions include the provision of timely data to inform leaders' decisionmaking; sufficient authority to reallocate people, time, and money; and resources according to students' needs. In Chapter Six, we explore conditions from the principals' perspective. Here, we provide information on how states and districts were attempting to improve data, autonomy, and resource conditions for school leaders.

Providing necessary data to inform leaders' decisionmaking. The majority of sites indicated that they had student-data systems in place and that they encouraged principals to use the data to make decisions. All states had systems that reported at least school-level state assessment results. Respondents, however, had different views on whether their systems provided sufficient, timely, and useful data. Some interviewees stated that their district had worked to provide data to principals by creating an interim assessment system. Others in the same district, however, reported that the system was an "antiquated pencil and paper system" that provided results six to eight weeks after the assessment, when students were already preparing for the next assessment.

At the time of our study, we found that some sites were actively attempting to make data more useful by improving alignment between curricula, standards, and assessments; reporting data at the individual student level; creating data-dashboards to facilitate comparison; and providing results of interim assessment data immediately. Iowa was in the process of developing an end-of-course assessment aligned with the new state curriculum and had recently started to provide state assessment results at the individual student level. Oregon had recently created an online adaptive state student assessment system that would provide teachers with instant results. Delaware was able to capitalize on its long-standing longitudinal data system and warehouse, and Massachusetts was in the process of launching such a system. States and districts were also providing additional types of data (such as survey data in Jefferson County), processes for collecting and analyzing data (such as the balanced scorecard strategic planning process in Delaware and Fort Wayne, school improvement planning processes in Fort Wayne and Springfield, MA, and walkthroughs in Kentucky and Portland),

and PD and/or technical assistance on how to analyze and use data (such as school improvement coaches in Springfield, IL, who guide data-driven decisionmaking).

Providing leaders with sufficient autonomy. We asked our interviewees to describe the policies and initiatives in their site that would affect principals' autonomy, i.e., initiatives that would have the effect of either expanding or limiting principals' authority.

Respondents differed in their opinion of whether levels of principal autonomy were problematic or not. Respondents from just fewer than 20 percent of the districts said that principals already had sufficient autonomy, suggesting that there was not a need for district or state policies to increase autonomy in their sites. However, respondents in 24 percent of districts told us that policies governing principal authority continued to be important impediments to principals' ability to be effective.

Twenty-four percent of the districts in our study had attempted to increase principal autonomy. For example, Boston had created a "pilot schools" program, in which schools apply to become pilot schools, where principals are given complete control over decisions regarding budgets, curriculum, and staffing.

Respondents in some of the sites indicated that there were problems regarding the success of their respective efforts to improve autonomy. For example, Massachusetts decided to replicate the Boston pilot schools program across the state. However, we were told that pilot school principals in Springfield had not received all of the promised autonomy. In Davenport, Iowa, the superintendent tried to modify the process by which teachers were assigned to schools to give principals more authority but was not able to make the required change to the teachers' contract. Interviewees in Indian River, Delaware, expressed concern that principals still do not have sufficient autonomy despite efforts to address these issues.

At least three states had attempted to influence principal autonomy indirectly by organizing training for school board members that encouraged them to focus on setting policy directions and discouraged them from interfering with decisions that principals should be making.

Allocating resources according to student needs. Three states and three districts had instituted weighted student formulas or other policies to allocate resources in accordance with student needs. Other sites were acting to improve resource conditions by allocating resources for additional leadership personnel, such as school administration managers (SAMs),[1] who assume traditional managerial responsibilities so that principals can reallocate their time in ways that better meet students' learning needs. Georgia created a $15,000-per-year salary incentive for high-performing principals to move to high-needs schools.

---

[1] The idea for and implementation of SAMs began in JCPS.

Comparison of Policies and Initiatives Across Sites

The policies and initiatives taken by the sites differed in focus, scope, stage of implementation, and the degree to which they challenged the status quo. We elaborate on these distinctions below.

Focus of Policies and Initiatives

Table 3.1 summarizes the widespread differences among initiatives in the sites we studied.[2] The most common policies and initiatives concerned standards (typically at the state level), pre-service and recruitment (typically at the district level), and in-service (at both the state and district levels). We found that a majority of the states were pursuing standards, the majority of districts were pursuing pre-service and recruitment policies and initiatives, and the majority of both states and districts were providing in-service support. These may have been the most common because they were the same sort of policies and initiatives that districts and states had pursued in the past, and they therefore experienced little resistance. Licensure policies were addressed only at the state level, and they were usually addressed via licensure restructuring. This finding was not surprising given that states are typically more likely than districts to have licensing authority. Most of the states did not pursue leader evaluation policies and initiatives, but most of the districts did. Again, this pattern may have simply indicated that districts are traditionally more likely than states to evaluate principals. Finally, sites varied considerably in the attention they were giving to improving certain conditions for leadership. About half of the states were working on providing necessary data to inform leaders' decisionmaking and targeting resources according to student needs, but fewer were focused on enhancing leader autonomy. Most districts were focused on providing necessary data, but fewer were pursuing efforts related to issues of providing autonomy or allocating targeted resources. This may have in part reflected the fact that state and district officials—and the broader education field—lack consensus on the extent and type of resources and autonomy principals need to be effective. Our respondents often offered differing views on this issue. If individual stakeholders have different visions of what is needed, this might affect their ability to work together to improve conditions.

Scope of Policies and Initiatives

Policies and initiatives differed not only in their focus, but also in their scope and ambition, as measured by the breadth of groups targeted by the actions, the number of initiatives pursued, and the number of people served by the initiatives.

---

[2] Separate results are not reported for aligned-system and leadership-network sites, because when we compared the types of policies and initiatives that were being pursued by these two types of sites, we did not find any differences. But the answers to our questions on how sites were attempting to improve conditions were not precise, which may have resulted in policies and actions appearing to be more similar than they really were.

Table 3.1
Differences Among District and State Policies and Initiatives to Improve Leadership

Policy/Initiative	States	Districts
Standards		
Setting systemwide standards	Majority of sites	Some sites
Updating standards	Majority of sites	Some sites
Broadening role groups	About half of sites	No sites
Pre-Service/Recruitment		
Sunsetting pre-service programs	Some sites	No sites
Collaborative redesign of pre-service programs	About half of sites	Some sites
Establishing or maintaining alternative pre-service programs	About half of sites	Majority of sites
Offering training and experiences aimed at increasing interest and knowledge about principalship	No sites	Some sites
Targeting recruitment efforts	Some sites	Majority of sites
Licensure		
Changing the licensure structure	Majority of sites	No sites
Creating licensure requirements	Some sites	No sites
Creating alternative licensure routes	Some sites	No sites
Evaluation		
Creating a common evaluation system	Some sites	Majority of sites
Creating or providing evaluation tools	Some sites	Some sites
Shifting the focus of evaluation to be more supportive of professional growth	Some sites	Some sites
In-service		
PD programs	Majority of sites	Majority of sites
Mentors	Majority of sites	Majority of sites
Coaches	Some sites	Some sites
Networks/professional learning communities	Majority of sites	Majority of sites
Conditions		
Providing necessary data to inform leaders' decisionmaking	About half of sites	Majority of sites
Providing leaders with sufficient autonomy	Some sites	Some sites
Allocating resources according to student needs	About half of sites	Some sites

Range of positions targeted by actions. Some policies and initiatives were more ambitious than others in that they were directed at a range of leadership personnel in addition to principals. Some actions targeted teacher leaders, school administrators, district officials, superintendents, and/or school board members. In general, teacher leaders were more likely to be targeted by pre-service efforts, and superintendents and district office staff were more likely to be targeted by in-service efforts. Some sites, including Massachusetts and Delaware, tended to pursue policies and initiatives that consistently targeted a broad range of personnel.

Comprehensiveness of actions. Some policies and initiatives were considered to be ambitious because they were components of a broader set of policies and initiatives that were bundled together. The first phase of the Wallace funding in Delaware was used to pursue a set of policies and initiatives that addressed several areas. These efforts included revising the licensure and certification system, adopting the ISLLC standards, funding a leader mentoring program and assessment center, revising the leader appraisal system, creating the annual Delaware Policy and Practice Institute, and expanding the Aspiring School Leader Internship Program. This was a much more comprehensive approach than that taken by Massachusetts, where the first phase of funding was primarily focused on one policy area, in-service development.

Number of people served. Some policies and initiatives attempted to reach greater numbers of people than others. This was particularly true of pre-service and in-service programs. One alternative district-based pre-service program served only 15 individuals, while another served 80. Similarly, some states offered PD programs that served between 50 and 100 participants. At the time of our study, the NISL program in Massachusetts had trained over 790 individuals. Some initiatives were offered only to a pilot group, while others were offered districtwide or statewide. For example, the Oregon Leadership Network (OLN) intentionally served teacher leaders, school leaders, central office leaders, state agency leaders, stakeholder leaders, and higher education leaders.

Stage of the Initiative

Some policies and initiatives were further along in implementation than others; some were still in the design stage, while others had been fully implemented for years. Several of the evaluation systems and tools, including DPAS II and VAL-ED, were being piloted at the time of our data collection. Similarly, some states had implemented statewide standards aligned with ISLLC standards only within the last year or two, while Delaware, for example, had had ISLLC standards in place since 2002. Some programs, such as Chicago's system of local school councils and Boston's pilot schools, have been in place for years. As such, some policies were more mature and had already had a significant impact on the way principals were recruited, prepared, and supported.

Challenge to the Status Quo

Policies and initiatives also varied in the amount of change they required. Some sites boldly challenged the status quo, while others went after what they called "low-hanging fruit." For example, the policy of sunsetting all pre-service programs in Iowa was an aggressive move that required substantive changes across many organizations within two years. Efforts to redesign pre-service programs in Massachusetts, on the other hand, did little to challenge the status quo. There, pre-service programs could voluntarily use a gap-analysis tool to self-identify areas where their program did not align with state standards for leadership. While our interview respondents hoped that all pre-service programs would eventually use the tool and revise their programs accordingly, this initiative was certainly less challenging to the status quo than a sunset policy that specified clear consequences for failure to act.

Conclusions

As we have shown, a great deal is being done at both the state and district levels in the sites we studied to improve policies and initiatives that influence instructional leadership, and states and districts appear equally capable of launching initiatives. Although states were more often responsible for certain policies, such as setting standards and licensure regulations, districts often took steps to influence those standards, set their own standards, or specify how state standards should be applied in their local context. We also found some signs that state and district roles may be converging. Some of the districts, for example, were entering into partnerships with universities to improve pre-service programming, a realm once confined to state authority. And some of the states had mandated mentoring for all new principals, a role traditionally assumed by district officials.

We made no attempt to evaluate the effectiveness of the initiatives but focused instead on describing what they were and how they differed across sites. According to the CLS hypothesis, a wide range of policies and initiatives must be in place before a CLS can be developed, and we found evidence that all the sites we studied had taken steps in this direction, although some pursued more reforms—and more wide-ranging reforms—than others. In the following three chapters, we describe how states and districts have worked together to create greater cohesion among these efforts. We begin by highlighting the different roles states and districts played in improving school leadership; we then analyze the levels of cohesion achieved in six sites; and finally, we describe the strategies and local contexts that appeared most conducive to system-building.

CHAPTER FOUR

Variations in State and District Roles in Improving School Leadership

Our investigation of whether states or districts tended to take the lead in efforts to improve school leadership found that districts took the lead in some cases, with little involvement from the state, and state agencies took the lead in other cases. Regardless of which pattern prevailed, some states were willing to identify and promote innovative efforts by what they termed "lead learner districts." In some sites, no clear leader had emerged. In Missouri and Rhode Island, for example, the districts' efforts at leadership improvement were limited, with few initiatives and therefore few scale-up opportunities. In Rhode Island, state agencies had seeded local innovation by funding district initiatives but had not yet created the infrastructure to monitor, evaluate, identify, or promote promising practices.

Districts as Leaders

Some larger districts developed their own leadership improvement initiatives with limited state oversight or involvement. Although district efforts could potentially lead to inefficiencies if multiple districts in a state design their own programs for such tasks as preparing new principals, district-led initiatives may be the only option in some states. Efforts by districts to lead school improvement initiatives appeared to stem from necessity, i.e., where the state had limited capacity to lead. These districts held leadership to be essential to broader school improvement efforts.

Two districts in particular, Atlanta and Fort Wayne, actively pursued leadership improvement before the state got involved. In both cases, the state played a limited supportive role and reportedly did not hinder district efforts. Within these two districts, leadership for school improvement initiatives was led by directors or managers of leader training and development. Indeed, in the majority of the study districts, efforts to improve school leadership were led by a director of professional development.

Fort Wayne Community Schools had taken up the mantra "leadership second only to instruction" and had invested considerable attention in developing school and district leaders. The emphasis on leadership was evidenced in all respondent interviews.

We also noted it while analyzing district leaders' presentations to the school board and the elaborate system they had implemented to support leader development. The cornerstone of this system was a series of leadership academies addressing the development of aspiring, novice, and practicing leaders. Fort Wayne Community Schools also aimed to influence the preparation of aspiring leaders through a partnership with Indiana University–Purdue University, Fort Wayne. The ongoing partnership between the district and the university sought to shape the curriculum to be responsive to the district's needs.

The Fort Wayne district embraced the notion of a cohesive leadership system at the district level by developing the Aligned System of Leadership Development standards, which were based on the state and ISLLC standards but enhanced to reflect an urban leadership context. The standards included a rubric that rated leadership behaviors at performance levels ranging from unacceptable to proficient and guided leader development and evaluation. The district also embraced a notion of distributive leadership and had created quality improvement teams that engaged teacher/staff leaders in a school improvement process that used the Balanced Scorecard tools. District leaders had worked closely with local stakeholders such as the principals' association, the teachers' union, and the school board to ensure a common focus on leadership and instructional improvement.

The district had had few interactions with the state regarding leadership improvement. The district tried to partner with state-level Wallace grantees earlier, but fragmented governance and turnover in grant leadership presented barriers to collaboration. In general, the district had ensured compliance with state requirements but had been pursuing its own leadership improvement initiatives, which the state did not direct.

The Atlanta Public Schools (APS) also functioned with little state support as the SEA rebuilt capacity after a period of tumultuous leadership under the previous chief state school officer (CSSO). At the time of our visit, the new CSSO had been successfully mending fractured relations between the SEA and other state agencies, as well as with districts. Nonetheless, Atlanta had largely gone about its own leadership improvement efforts as part of its vision for improving district performance.

Atlanta's superintendent has had the support and backing of her board in her pursuit of reforms. In this right-to-work state, teachers' and principals' organizations have not objected to actions that in other states might have been more problematic, in particular, the firing of many staff. Most notably, the APS superintendent changed the district culture concerning both leadership—people came to understand that leadership positions had to be earned—and accountability—leaders at all levels understood that poor performance could cause them to lose their positions. The superintendent's actions in her early years reinforced these messages: Principals who did not demonstrate commitment to the district's vision and/or consistently failed to meet student learning targets were removed. The district introduced a school performance intervention process that principals had to agree to if their school was not meeting performance targets. Principals who did not buy into the district's vision and make efforts to improve could be removed. In addition, they would be removed if they consistently failed to meet performance targets despite interventions and district support. APS interviewees reported that improving school leadership was a critical lever for meeting the district's student performance goals. Only those school leaders who were willing to meet these goals and capable of doing so had been encouraged to remain. We were told in an interview that 89 percent of principals had left since the current superintendent arrived; many had decided to retire, but others were removed over the years for not meeting performance targets. Principals who were removed were not reassigned; once the district dismissed them for poor performance, they could not assume another principalship.

The superintendent also initiated a number of structural reforms and programs to build school leadership capacity. She created school reform teams (SRTs), leadership groups responsible for student outcomes in clusters of 14 to 22 schools. Each SRT included a group of educational coaches and model teacher leaders with subject-specific expertise, and all focused on supporting instructional leadership. The district also put principal performance targets in place and had issued a set of 26 best teaching practices that formed the basis of principal instructional support. The district also ran a superintendent's academy for people who already had principal certification, designed "to increase the leadership quotient of the principals we already have." In general, principals received a wide range of PD, including monthly SRT training, an annual leadership retreat, focused training on data use provided by the Research, Planning and Accountability Office, and a mentor in their first three years on the job.

To address the district's need for future school leaders, APS established the Aspiring Leaders Program, a one-year program for working teachers who wished to attain a leadership position. This program led to certification and was jointly administered with Georgia State University. The Superintendent's Academy for Building Leaders in Education was developed by APS for people who already had principal certification. This program was designed "to increase the leadership quotient of the principals we already have," emphasizing key elements of leadership, such as team-building, data-based decisionmaking, and strategic planning.

Atlanta's leadership framework is improved upon each year. Interviewees noted that leadership improvement is a process, and each year builds on what they learned the year before.

States as Leaders

In Delaware and Iowa, leadership improvement efforts were primarily state-led, although districts were often involved in planning committees or working groups. Districts in these states were not receiving funding from The Wallace Foundation, which may have served to elevate the state's role.

In both states, leadership for the CLS work was spread over multiple organizations. In Iowa, the placement of the Wallace grantee of record in the administrators' association propelled the association to a new level of activity in pursuing leadership improvement. The School Administrators of Iowa took the lead in developing leadership standards and modules for evaluating school leaders and superintendents, and through the grant resources, provided funding for programs such as SAMs. The Iowa CSSO was a highly capable leader who was credited with pushing for the redesign of the administrator pre-service system. The Iowa SEA was prominently involved in leadership initiatives to improve school leadership as well. Most, but not all, interviewees in Iowa credited the SEA with having had capacity to spearhead school leadership initiatives, including either strong leadership or access to resources, or both.[1] The SEA was proactive in ensuring that its 10 area education agencies were supporting school leaders. In Delaware, a university played a key leadership role, providing legitimacy and nonpartisan leadership on school improvement initiatives. The Delaware SEA was active in creating data systems for leaders, developing school improvement processes, and linking Wallace-funded leadership reforms with other state leadership initiatives, such as Vision 2015.[2] In both Delaware and Iowa, legislatures played key roles by putting in place requirements and provisions (and often state funding) for mentoring, evaluation, and induction of new administrators.

Iowa designed and worked at scale, focusing attention on policies and practices that would influence all districts. The state resolved that university-based leader preparation programs needed to be redesigned to place more emphasis on instructional leadership and the new Iowa Standards for School Leaders. As described above, the CSSO decided to sunset these programs, requiring them to reapply for approval. The state also required the area education agencies to provide evidence of support to leadership development.

Delaware identified two "breakthrough ideas"—succession planning and distributed leadership—and created a competitive mini-grants program to seed district programs to address them. Appoquinimink, Christina, and Indian River used this seed

---

[1] As a point of comparison, we found that interviewees in the less-cohesive states were more likely to report housing their CLS efforts primarily in SEAs with what they described as low levels of resources, including insufficient personnel.

[2] Vision 2015 is a statewide education reform effort cosponsored by the Business Roundtable and the Delaware Department of Education. The Vision 2015 report challenged the education system to implement seven recommendations ranging from improving the curriculum to supporting school leaders and adopting a student-weighted funding formula for school finance. Vision 2015 worked with the Delaware Academy for School Leadership to launch a school network to implement the Vision 2015 recommendations in an ever-expanding group of schools and districts.

funding to develop and implement programs to identify and train promising aspiring leader candidates. A variety of statewide forums provided all 19 districts in the state with opportunities to learn about these promising practices and subsequent opportunities to apply for seed funding. Similarly, Delaware sought to promote distributed leadership by funding several districts to develop pilot initiatives. The districts were required to waive any school board, central office, or teachers' union policy barriers to creating a more distributed leadership system. The Delaware CLS tracked these waivers and used the CLS-initiated annual statewide policy and practice institute to share the pilot models across the state. In general, Delaware focused on a set of ready and willing districts, while simultaneously promoting innovative practices throughout the state.

Iowa and Delaware, like most other sites with state-led efforts, employed some mandates in an effort to influence district practice throughout the state. But the mandates varied in the extent to which district practices were specified. For example, Iowa and Delaware both enacted leader evaluation policies. Iowa mandated that all principals and superintendents be evaluated on the basis of state standards, with an emphasis on progress on meeting individualized growth plans. However, districts were permitted to develop their own assessment tools. In contrast, Delaware mandated the use of a particular assessment, DPAS II, which required that administrators set goals, gather and document evidence of progress toward goals through completion of specified forms and surveys, and participate in a number of required conferences with evaluators.

While Delaware and Iowa were notable in their state-led approach to promoting leadership improvement practices at the district level, other states also followed this approach, to varying degrees. District responses to state mandates depended on the nature of the efforts and whether they supplemented or supplanted district efforts. A Boston leader noted that the state's required mentoring or induction for new principals helped to legitimize and institutionalize these supports. In describing the state role, she noted:

> Before, if you could do it [support new principals], you did. But if you couldn't, so what? . . . The attitude was "it's a great idea and if we can afford it we do it." But [when it was mandated], they [districts] don't have a choice.

States Promoting District Initiatives

If a state can capitalize on and spread district innovation, districts can benefit from each other and reduce inefficiencies. However, the willingness and ability of states in our study to recognize and scale up successful district practices to make them more widely available varied.

In Kentucky, most of the state leadership initiatives originated in the work of JCPS. JCPS and four local principal preparation providers agreed on a framework for principal preparation based on a co-design/co-delivery model that would better meet the district's needs. State officials saw this as an opportunity to radically change the way leadership preparation was being provided throughout the state. The state also worked collaboratively with JCPS to scale up the SAMs program and the Instructional Leadership Team network described above.

Other states reported capitalizing on district initiatives as well. Georgia considers APS its lead learner district and often looks to APS as an incubator of programs and ideas. State support for SAMs grew out of APS's experiments with the program. In Oregon, OLN has served as a vehicle for scale-up activities. In Illinois, Chicago and Springfield interviewees reported that the Illinois State Action for Education Leadership Project (IL-SAELP) leaders had learned from and capitalized on district programs, such as mentoring and other PD programs for early career principals, to improve school leadership.

Conclusions

We found that both states and districts were capable of leading efforts to improve school leadership. The districts that were strong leaders tended to be large urban districts with the resources and personnel to assume the lead without support from the state. They also had direct funding and technical assistance from The Wallace Foundation. With that support, they were able to align their leadership improvement efforts around locally developed standards, create partnerships with local universities, and, in some cases, gain permission from their states to certify leaders through their own preparation programs.

We found few instances, however, of district initiatives spreading to other districts without state intervention. States were the most effective agents in ensuring that promising practices were spread to other districts. State actors were also able to influence widespread change by using their legislative powers, such as mandating the reform of all principal preparation programs. States were able to spur action in districts by providing incentives to take on leadership improvement efforts, as happened in Delaware, where districts were given incentives to introduce distributed leadership systems in their schools. States were also in a better position to establish systems of distributed leadership for the CLS work. In Delaware and Iowa, state leadership was highly distributed, with political actors (e.g., legislatures), professional actors (e.g., CSSOs and SEAs), and supporting actors (e.g., universities and professional associations) all playing key roles. This distribution across multiple capable actors probably helped the states gain wide buy-in for their work and allowed them to use multiple strategies to improve school leadership, such as mandating change, communicating the importance of change across multiple stakeholder groups, and providing symbolic legitimacy for leadership improvement initiatives.

We also found that the nature of the interaction between states and districts sometimes changed over time. The new state superintendent in Georgia, for example, recognized the achievements in Atlanta and, at the time of our study, viewed it as a lead learner district. Georgia will likely begin to disseminate Atlanta's best practices across the state, thereby making it a site with both state- and district-led efforts. In Kentucky, the state and a district had also become equal co-leads in leadership improvement efforts.

CHAPTER FIVE

Building Cohesion Across Policies and Initiatives

We have defined CLSs as a comprehensive set of leadership policies and actions aligned within and across systems, developed through a coordinated process that engages diverse stakeholders who reached agreement on a set of actions to address school leadership. In this chapter, we analyze the extent to which selected sites have developed such systems. We focus on six of the sites the Foundation identified as having made the most progress toward developing a CLS: Delaware, Georgia, Illinois, Iowa, Kentucky, and Massachusetts. We also draw contrasts with non-CLS sites: Fort Wayne Community Schools, Indiana, Missouri (including St. Louis Public Schools), Oregon (including Eugene and Portland Public Schools), Providence Public Schools, andRhode Island.

The purpose of this part of the analysis is to provide a better understanding of the work that goes into building these systems. We distinguish the most-advanced sites from less-advanced sites to identify the strategies and contextual factors associated with the fullest achievement of CLSs. These comparative assessments are snapshots in time, coinciding with our site visits (March to November 2008), and not evaluations of the potential for progress in each site. The states and districts we studied were at different points in their leadership development work, and there was evidence to suggest that the sites identified as less advanced at the time of the site visits were on their way to developing stronger CLSs.

We begin with a review of the literature that helped us develop a framework for understanding the dimensions of CLSs. We then compare the sites along five dimensions of a CLS based on our analyses of interviews with stakeholders and documents collected from interviewees and the Foundation.

Dimensions of Cohesion

For several decades, the problem of policy and programmatic coherence has been a central focus in discussions of systemic school reform. Programs at the federal, state, and local levels often send contradictory messages, and few opportunities exist for local policymakers to work together (Fuhrman, 1993). Responding to pressure for improved student performance, states, districts, and schools have taken on a multitude of improvement initiatives that have strained the capacity of local educators to coordinate and implement programs (Bryk et al., 1998; Hatch, 2002). Incoherence is linked to a number of inefficiencies and/or negative outcomes. For example, elementary schools pursue multiple initiatives as a way to garner important organizational resources, but lack of coordination and coherence limits their potential for positive results and fragments educator attention (Newmann et al., 2001). The Wallace Foundation has argued that lack of cohesion in leadership policies and practices—both within and between the different levels of public education—undermines school leaders' abilities to achieve learning improvements (The Wallace Foundation, 2006).

Building coherence suggests a systemic approach to educational improvement in which stakeholders and governing authorities work "in harmony and synergistically" to address the collective challenges faced by states, districts, and schools (Unger et al., 2008). Coherence traditionally implies alignment of policies and practices, or at least the absence of obvious policy conflict. Coherent education policies should send the same messages, avoid contradictions, and "build on one another in some way to form a larger whole" (Fuhrman, 1993). When states and districts launch systemic efforts to improve school leadership, the degree of coherence among policies and initiatives is likely to influence the attainment of such goals.

In contrast to the structural perspective on coherence, which emphasizes alignment, there is also a process approach to achieving coherence. Honig and Hatch (2004) argue that policy coherence, in the sense of alignment, is not an inherently positive (or negative) condition. They reframe the idea of coherence as a dynamic process by which organizations strategically use external demands to strengthen their performance, arguing that schools and school districts should work in partnership to negotiate the fit between external demands and organizational goals. In this view, coherence is a social construction produced through continual interactions among a range of stakeholders in education, and incoherent policy messages may provide an opportunity for educational organizations to craft a response that fits their local needs.

The process perspective emphasizes that engagement of stakeholders provides opportunities for the negotiation of meaning and supports policy implementation in a way that gives participants a deeper understanding of the nature of the change required by a new policy or practice (Spillane, 2000). With respect to leadership development, Young, Petersen, and Short (2002) call for the creation of an alliance of practitioners, professional associations, educational leadership faculty, university leaders, authorizing agencies, and others to engage in the preparation of educational leaders.

Attempting to change standard practices or policies invariably creates conflict among competing interest groups. Bolman and Deal (2003, p. 378) note that "successful change requires an ability to frame issues, build coalitions, and establish arenas in which disagreements can be forged into workable pacts." Conflict is managed through bargaining and negotiation where agreements can be crafted. Public arenas then become generative in the change process as they provide forums within which agreement can be reached. Agreement is an indicator of the extent to which productive negotiation regarding goals and strategies has occurred (Madda, Halverson, and Gomez, 2007).

Successful cross-stakeholder initiatives require work to coordinate individual and group efforts with systemwide goals. By *coordination*, we mean active work to integrate diverse elements into a harmonious operation. The importance of coordination is noted in the research on public administration, particularly social service delivery and policy implementation requiring interorganizational networks (see, for example, Provan and Milward, 1995). Coordination, through the actions of a leader or convener, is an important component of successful collaborative work (Legler and Reischl, 2003).

Drawing on this literature, we conclude that cohesive leadership systems are characterized by the following dimensions:

Structural
- *Comprehensiveness* of policies and initiatives, addressing the types of policies and initiatives described in Chapter Three (standards, pre-service and recruitment, licensure, evaluation, in-service, and improving conditions)
- *Alignment* of policies and practices within and between levels of the system (state and district)

Process
- *Engagement* of relevant stakeholders in the development and implementation of policies and initiatives
- *Agreement* among stakeholders regarding the salience of school leadership and how to improve it
- *Coordination* that promotes alignment, engagement, and agreement around leadership development initiatives.

The remainder of this chapter presents our findings, organized by the five dimensions of cohesion. We highlight the status of the six CLS sites on each dimension, and when possible, we compare their status to that of non-CLS sites.

Variation in Implementing Cohesive Leadership Systems

The cohesiveness of leadership systems in the six CLS sites varied at the time of our study. We found the most variation on the structural dimensions of cohesion and relatively little variation on the process dimensions.

Comprehensive Leadership Policies and Initiatives

We include comprehensiveness as a component of a cohesive leadership system to underscore the argument that cohesion in and of itself may not be fruitful. We expect that a site building a system to improve school leadership will have implemented a set of comprehensive policies to address the continuum of a leader's career (from standards and pre-service programming to evaluation, in-service, and conditions). Although we cannot conclude that these policies are the "right" ones, we still credit the sites that are attempting to improve school leadership through multiple levers. Overall, our analysis suggests that Delaware, Iowa, and Kentucky had the most comprehensive systems of leadership development policies and practices. These three states had attended to standards, licensure, pre-service, in-service, evaluation, and conditions. The remaining three CLS states had addressed fewer components of the system and/or had addressed a particular component with less ambitious policies or initiatives.

The policies and practices enacted by the Iowa CLS project exemplify a comprehensive system of leadership development. Recently elaborated leader standards specified desired leader behaviors. Aspiring leaders participated in redesigned preparation programs that included coursework and clinical experiences tailored to the realities of leading schools. A two-tiered licensure system required that novice administrators be monitored and assessed on the basis of the leader standards and that novices receive support from mentors and induction programs at the district level. An extensive set of PD offerings coordinated through the Iowa Leadership Academy targeted leaders at different career stages. Iowa CLS grantees were instrumental in the adoption of a policy requiring that all principals and superintendents be evaluated using the leadership standards, with emphasis on progress toward goals established in individualized growth plans. And a coalition of state agencies sought to influence the conditions that shape leader effectiveness, with attention to redefining leader roles, responsibilities, and authority. Iowa's Urban Education Network supported the work of eight large districts in redesigning their central offices to better support principal leadership. Iowa was also experimenting with the use of SAMs who assume school management duties to free principals' time to support instructional improvement and teacher development.

Throughout the Wallace grant period, the Delaware CLS grantees also made significant strides in creating a comprehensive leadership development system. By the end of the first phase of the SAELP program (in 2004), Delaware had revised its licensure and certification system for educators, adopted the ISLLC standards, funded a leader mentoring program and diagnostic assessment center, established an annual statewide forum for addressing leader policy and practice, created "skills and knowledge clusters" or PD modules that provide leaders with salary increases to incentivize participation, redesigned its three leader preparation programs through a critical friends review process, and revised the leader evaluation system (implemented statewide in 2008–2009). Following these achievements, the second phase of work focused on two "breakthrough ideas," succession planning and distributed leadership. The succession planning work was piloted in a group of districts developing a pool of aspiring school leaders who had the skills, knowledge, and disposition to take on leadership roles as positions become available. The distributed leadership initiative, aimed primarily at middle and high schools, sought to provide teachers with opportunities and training to assume leadership roles in those schools. When we studied Delaware, the CLS leaders were aiming to increase the number of districts participating in the two breakthrough strategies, while deepening opportunities for training and development.

Like Iowa and Delaware, Kentucky had a system in place that included a broad set of policies and initiatives. The Kentucky CLS coalition represented a collaborative effort between JCPS and the Kentucky Department of Education. Jefferson County took the early lead in developing a number of policies and practices, including the creation of a "continuum" that specified standards for principal practice across stages of development (novice to professional), formed partnerships with local universities to redesign preparation programs, developed instructional leadership teams at the school level, and piloted a SAM position at some schools.

Kentucky had not yet addressed evaluation of acting principals beyond a state requirement that districts evaluate principals on the basis of the standards; however, principal candidates had to pass a standards-based assessment. Jefferson County evaluated principals through a portfolio-based process, and principals set growth targets based on district and school goals, gathered evidence of their progress toward those goals, and met with supervisors several times each year to revisit their professional growth plans.

While Delaware, Iowa, and Kentucky had the most-advanced CLSs at the time of our study, other CLS grantees had also taken significant steps. Massachusetts had invested significant resources in and attention to ongoing PD for acting leaders. Approximately 800 principals had participated in NISL training—a sustained and intensive learning opportunity. Other components of the Massachusetts CLS were under development, including revised standards and a new licensure system.

Illinois focused primarily on licensure, mentoring for new principals, and evaluation; more work was needed to support more-experienced leaders and to address pre-service preparation. Chicago and Springfield addressed these gaps locally by emphasizing in-service and partnering with local pre-service providers.

Georgia focused on early-career leaders by defining performance-based leader standards and by beginning to implement ambitious new requirements for preparation programs, including a supervised residency and co-design and implementation with districts. Both the Georgia Leadership Institute for School Improvement (GLISI) and the APS invested heavily in in-service programs. Overall, Georgia was in the process of addressing most system components, but a number of its initiatives, such as updating the licensure system and developing a leader evaluation tool, were in the development stage.

Alignment of Policies and Practices Within and Across Levels

Delaware, Iowa, and Kentucky carefully designed and implemented their CLSs to ensure alignment within and across levels of the system. Interviewees in these states were able to articulate strong alignment among the various policies and initiatives promoted by the CLS. The three states also worked to ensure that leadership initiatives were aligned with broader educational reform aims. A state educational leader in Iowa explained:

> Alignment is really important to us; we do want everything aligned. Even before the leadership initiative, our focus was to have everything aligned under school improvement to increase student achievement. That remains today, except that leadership is now an important piece.

In all three states, standards provided the anchor for alignment. A participant in the Delaware CLS work noted that the state standards guide leader support throughout the career continuum:

> We adopted the ISLLC standards and not just that, but what made it cohesive is that, from start to finish, from pre-service to induction to career, the ISLLC are the focus of professional development and evaluation.

The Iowa Standards for School Leaders form the basis for accreditation of preparation programs, the content of mentoring and induction programs for novice leaders, and the evaluation of principals and superintendents. Kentucky adopted the national ISLLC standards but further elaborated the characteristics of effective principals through the creation of what they called the continuum, which guided preparation program redesign and, increasingly, PD offerings. In both Iowa and Kentucky, existing preparation programs were reformed, and redesigned programs were required to demonstrate alignment with standards.

Delaware exemplified alignment in a number of novel ways. Once CLS leaders identified distributed leadership as a "breakthrough idea," the CLS group worked with higher education faculty to ensure that a distributed model of leadership was promoted in pre-service programs. They also aligned their approach to mentoring across initiatives. State leaders involved in the CLS grant developed a pool of mentors and coaches who were trained at the New York Leadership Academy and supported first-year principals and participants in the distributed leadership and Vision 2015 initiatives. Finally, teachers were introduced to the concept of distributed leadership through the teacher version of the state evaluation system, which required them to identify goals related to taking on leadership roles in their schools.

In some CLS sites, we rated alignment as less advanced, because components of the system were still under development. For example, Massachusetts had leadership standards in place, but they were not yet used as the basis for leader evaluation or pre-service preparation programs.

Among CLS sites with less alignment, state mandates were to some extent a source of alignment conflict in districts that already had established practices. For example, although the Illinois legislation on evaluation and mentoring borrowed from Chicago and Springfield district practices, Springfield had to revise its evaluation and mentoring policies to abide by the new state law. District officials and principals reported that some changes were advantageous, while others were less so. Under the state legislation, a mentor had to have a minimum of three years' experience as a successful principal. Principals we interviewed in Springfield noted frustration with this requirement, because it limited the pool of potential mentors. Some mentors had ample experience and success as district administrators, but this experience was not relevant under the state legislation.

Some pre-service programs remained poorly aligned because of limited state and district influence. Four of the six CLS sites had taken steps to improve pre-service preparation, and districts were working directly with local preparation programs in the sites with little state-level action. Both Chicago and Springfield (IL) had strong linkages with local preparation programs (a combination of university-based and alternative programs) that predated state-level initiatives. However, considerable work remained to be done in most sites to link pre-service preparation to state standards and particularly to district needs. A respondent in Illinois said:

> They [higher education] seem to be trying to keep this ivory tower mentality. We are trying to get them to recognize that the school district is [their] client. It is not the district providing you people to keep your program going. There is a disconnect between what districts need and what programs provide.

In the non-CLS sites, alignment among leadership improvement policies and initiatives varied. In most cases, there was evidence of only limited alignment (between a few leadership actions), and in some cases, there was little alignment at all. For example, there was little alignment among leadership improvement actions in Rhode Island, because the state had employed a strategy of funding a range of programs within districts that operated as demonstration sites. We are not certain why other states made less progress in aligning their actions across the state and with partner districts. Interviewees in these states reported either that their SEA was focused on rural districts, making it difficult to align initiatives with urban districts; that their state had a history of a culture of independence that worked against alignment; or that their governor did not support the efforts to improve school leadership, which stymied progress. These barriers are explored more fully in Chapter Six.

Engagement of Stakeholders

Most CLS sites achieved broad stakeholder engagement in the development and implementation of their CLSs. Delaware, Georgia, Illinois, Iowa, and Kentucky assembled broad-reaching coalitions to engage state- and local-level leaders, to raise the salience of school leadership on the education reform agenda, and, at times, to actively contribute to the design and implementation of specific policies and initiatives. Respondents in these states were less apt to report that critical stakeholders had not been involved in the leadership improvement work.

Most CLS sites assembled a consortium of stakeholders to address requirements in their Wallace grant. Kentucky's Education Leadership Development Consortium met monthly with representatives from higher education institutions, state agencies, professional associations, and other groups, with a mission to "advance student learning through a collaborative focus on leadership development." Iowa formed the Leadership Partnership, which met quarterly to provide input and guidance on the feasibility of proposed policies and initiatives to support school leaders.

Delaware formed a consortium during the early SAELP work and also hosted an annual forum for engaging a very broad group of stakeholders in leadership development work, the Delaware Policy and Practice Institute. At this annual conference, the Institute highlighted promising practices in pilot districts (e.g., succession planning and distributed leadership) and engaged stakeholders in conversations to determine and prioritize the needs for future work.

Massachusetts also formed a broad coalition—the Education Leadership Alliance—that included professional organizations, service providers, and the Department of Education to design and deliver leadership services. The Alliance had partnerships with professional associations representing school committees (school boards), superintendents, and elementary and secondary principals' associations. However, engagement was rated lower in Massachusetts because several respondents noted that an important stakeholder—higher education—was generally not involved. Perhaps because the Alliance started with a focus on in-service for leaders, it had chosen not to involve higher education in the state's early leadership development work; however, when it expanded its focus to include standards development and possibly pre-service redesign, working with higher education became more important. The challenge was how to engage a community of such size and prestige with its 35 school leadership preparation programs. Although the higher education institutions had opportunities for input via focus groups and professional associations, the sheer number of programs made it difficult to get stakeholders at the same table for productive interaction. Other states, such as Kentucky, with 11 pre-service providers, or Delaware, with only three, did not face such challenges.

While most CLS sites had broad stakeholder engagement in their leadership development work, the extent to which stakeholders were involved varied. For example, governors (or their staffs) and state boards of education were often aware of the work and perhaps attended a few meetings but, not surprisingly, were less often involved in sustained interaction around initiative design. Nonetheless, symbolic involvement of high-level political leaders was viewed by professional staff as instrumental in the success of initiatives. For example, a Kentucky coalition team member noted that the governor's office supported the state's leadership development work by welcoming participants at high-profile events and by lending support for the passage of key legislative actions.

Stakeholder Agreement

To move a leadership agenda forward, stakeholder coalitions must achieve some level of agreement about strategy. Five states—Delaware, Georgia, Iowa, Kentucky, and Massachusetts—were particularly successful in meeting this goal. Reaching agreement on policies and initiatives that support leader development was an active process managed by project leaders. Faced with an initial lack of agreement from universities (particularly university leaders) regarding preparation program redesign, a cross-stakeholder group in Kentucky worked to overcome opposition. Now all 11 universities in the state have agreed to the key tenets of redesign work. While some elements, such as redesign to align with the state's leadership continuum, were supported by regulation, others required voluntary agreement. For example, all 11 universities have committed to using a common set of anchor assessments.

Illinois achieved agreement in some areas of leadership improvement, but not in others. It was reported to be difficult in Illinois to reach agreement between universities and the K–12 sector. One respondent said, "The higher education sector has to understand that their initiatives work together with what everyone else is trying to do." However, CLS leaders in the state managed to gain widespread consensus on their core legislative package, and it was unanimously approved by the state legislature.

The non-CLS sites had mixed levels of agreement. A notable example is Oregon, where the SEA, CSSO, and district leaders in Eugene and Portland shared a strong vision of developing culturally competent school leaders. The focus on cultural competency was a central tenet of much of their leadership development work, and through OLN, these organizations worked with an increasing number of districts over the years. On the other hand, Rhode Island's General Assembly, Board of Regents, and Department of Education/CSSO were all influential in setting education policy, yet they lacked agreement regarding strategy and focus for education reform. In addition, the governor's education reform agenda differed significantly from that of the SEA.

Coordination

All CLS sites had structures in place to coordinate their work, and this was one of the factors that distinguished CLS sites from non-CLS sites. By *coordination*, we mean the presence of an individual or agency taking a lead role in fostering stakeholder engagement, agreement, and an aligned system of leadership policies and initiatives. In sites with strong coordination, the agency receiving the Wallace grant played a coordinating role. In Delaware, there was broad engagement, but a small group at the Delaware Academy for School Leadership provided the coordination and strategic planning, with help from an external consultant. In Massachusetts, a few individuals within the Department of Education coordinated the work. In Kentucky, state and JCPS district leaders jointly did most of the coordinating.

In many cases, respondents identified the SAELP or CLS project director as a critical coordinator. In Delaware, Illinois, Iowa, and Kentucky, numerous respondents reported the image of the SAELP/CLS director delivering all the relevant stakeholders "to the same table." A state leader in Kentucky described a state coordinator of the Kentucky coalition as follows:

> She is key in all of this: her leadership and her ability to bring people together, bring them to the table, is amazing. She has been able to, which just floors me, . . . get university people to the table and sit down together and talk about their programs with the standards board, with KDE [Kentucky Department of Education] people, so I think it's been huge. It's one of those situations where you had the right person, at the right time, in the right place. So she's been working at combining her work with the Kentucky Leadership Academy, with the standards board, with the universities; it's this octopus but it is all so interrelated and interconnected with every other agency. So that to me is the way it needs to happen.

Similarly, the CLS leader in Iowa was described as "great at clarifying what we wanted to create and keeping our preferred future in front of us." And Delaware's CLS director was described as a "wonderful leader," "one of those truly gifted people," and someone with "extraordinary vision," who is both a "big-picture person" and also the "nuts-and-bolts person."

Coordination was somewhat more complex in Georgia, where two groups coordinated the leadership work. GLISI had been an important player in driving the leadership agenda. The governor proposed the formation of GLISI, which includes the Board of Regents, the business community, and other key education stakeholders. Funding for GLISI's work is supported by local foundations, the state, and the Board of Regents. GLISI is not a traditional coordinating agency. One interviewee described it as "less like an institution and more like a movement." As such, some respondents viewed GLISI as "boutique," because it focused on a small number of partner districts. Leaders in GLISI felt they did not have a choice; without any structural authority to intervene, GLISI must "work with willing leaders." As such, the coordination that GLISI provided differed considerably from that provided in Iowa, where the highest levels of state political leadership played a strong coordinating role.

Another potential coordinating group in Georgia, the Alliance of Education Agency Heads, was led by the CSSO and included the heads of key state agencies and institutions, including the university system, the professional standards commission, the state office of school achievement, and local school districts. However, this alliance's ability to coordinate leadership development work was reportedly limited, in part by its large size and the lack of involvement of district superintendents.

In the non-CLS sites, there was less coordination between the state and districts. In one non-CLS site, the state and one district had achieved some coordination on a single initiative—a series of statewide cultural competency conferences—but coordination for leadership development work outside of this one activity was limited, and virtually nonexistent when the initiative ended. In several non-CLS sites, coordination between state action and the work of large districts was strained because of the perception among urban districts that the state did not understand their needs. There was also a history of discord between the state and a large urban district in one site, reports that the governor did not support the work in another site, and a culture of independence in two of the non-CLS sites that may have impeded the ability of any one group to assume a coordinating role.

Conclusions

Overall, Delaware, Iowa, and Kentucky had the most-advanced CLSs (see Table 5.1). These three sites, which had comprehensive and aligned systems, were also more likely to have higher levels of engagement, agreement, and coordination than the other CLS sites, with the exception of Georgia. The fact that Georgia ranked high on the three process dimensions may suggest that it was poised to enact a comprehensive and aligned system. The other two CLS sites, Illinois and Massachusetts, were relatively weaker on one of the process dimensions of cohesion. The Massachusetts CLS team needed to find ways to engage the higher education community in order to continue to advance its leadership agenda. And CLS efforts in Illinois would likely have benefited from continuing to address stakeholder agreement to support pre-service program reform.

Table 5.1
Site Variation in CLS Development and Implementation

| State | Structural Dimensions of Cohesion | | Process Dimensions of Cohesion | | |
	Comprehensiveness	Alignment	Engagement	Agreement	Coordination
Delaware	More	More	More	More	More
Georgia	Less	Less	More	More	More
Illinois	Less	Less	More	Less	More
Iowa	More	More	More	More	More
Kentucky	More	More	More	More	More
Massachusetts	Less	Less	Less	More	More

Although we have discussed each dimension of cohesion separately, it is important to note that they are mutually reinforcing and in many ways more related than separate. One participant in Illinois offered an example of interrelated engagement and alignment:

> The Illinois State Board of Education [ISBE] and the Illinois Board of Higher Education [IBHE] impact [leader] preparation in different ways; the state board oversees the certification, but the IBHE oversees programs and how they approve these programs. . . . Now both state agencies are in meetings together. That is something they didn't do before. In fact, the ISBE and IBHE jointly created the school leadership task force.

While the work of these two agencies is interdependent, there was little interaction before the CLS work began. This example illustrates the way Illinois engaged key stakeholders and also provided an opportunity for aligning the work of agencies responsible for different aspects of leader preparation.

We identified tension in some dimensions of cohesion. Our analysis suggests that it can be difficult to promote broad stakeholder engagement and at the same time achieve agreement among diverse participants. The case of Indiana is illustrative. Indiana achieved high levels of stakeholder engagement in the early years of its Wallace grant by assembling the Indiana Promise Consortium. The Promise Consortium included the CSSO, the governor, representatives from the General Assembly, a member of the Indiana Board of Education, state education associations, higher education institutions, PD agencies, the business community, school leaders, and Indiana Department of Education staff members. In addition, throughout Indiana's leadership development work on licensure reform, pre-service redesign, and PD, lead agencies assembled cross-role working groups and provided opportunities to vet proposed practices with a wider audience. For example, members of the Office of Educator Licensure and Development's School Leaders Committee held meetings in four regions of the state to get feedback on the proposed (now adopted) two-tiered licensure system.

However, Indiana's experience also displays how broad stakeholder engagement may be a threat to cohesion in that the broader the group, the more difficult it is to achieve and maintain agreement on policies and initiatives. When reflecting on the Promise Consortium's work, one member said, "There were a lot of reasons why a lot of work was not as productive as it could have been, because of our great attempt at inclusion." Participants in the broad agenda of the Promise Consortium noted that stakeholders with strong interests made it difficult to agree on concrete actions. Smaller stakeholder groups that formed around specific issues, such as licensure reform and pre-service program redesign, were more easily able to reach agreement and enact specific policies.

Even when CLS sites achieved broad engagement and relatively high levels of agreement, tension was present. A stakeholder in Iowa commented, "The Leadership

Partnership group is so huge, a good group to bring in for information and brainstorming, but where is the table for making decisions?" This comment suggests that CLSs might benefit from a combination of forums promoting broad stakeholder engagement and settings where decisions and agreement can be hashed out in smaller groups, as exemplified by Illinois and Delaware.

We found that states are better positioned than districts to foster broad stakeholder engagement and agreement among stakeholders, coordinate initiatives, and ensure alignment among resulting policies throughout the state. State agencies are also more aware of other education reforms and how to integrate leadership improvements into the broader agenda.

Although states played the key role in achieving CLSs, some districts in the less-advanced CLS sites accomplished significant leadership improvement at the district level, as described in Chapter Four. Some districts developed systems that addressed a broad and aligned set of leadership improvement policies and initiatives supported by a coordinated effort to engage and reach agreement among stakeholders. There was strong evidence of district-level progress in Atlanta and Springfield (IL). This was even the case within the non-CLS group. For example, Fort Wayne Community Schools implemented its own leadership development system. It is important, however, to distinguish districtwide achievements from the CLS hypothesis, in which states and districts are expected to work together to develop aligned policies and initiatives.

In the next chapter, we take a close look at the strategies used to build CLSs, focusing particularly on Delaware, Iowa, and Kentucky.

CHAPTER SIX

Effective Strategies for System-Building

This chapter highlights the strategies used by sites to build support for policies and initiatives to improve school leadership and create greater cohesion among state and district efforts. We focus primarily on states, which we found to be the key agents in this work, but we reference district work as well. We were particularly interested in learning how three of the sites achieved relatively advanced systems.

We begin with a brief discussion of the growing role of the state in education policy and school reform, to place our finding that states tended to take the lead in building CLSs in context. Then we describe the strategies most commonly used by all the sites in developing a systematic approach to improving school leadership policy and practice, distinctive features in the approach of the three most advanced sites, and local contexts that appeared to support or inhibit such work.

Growing Importance of the State

State organizations are in the best position to build statewide cohesion around education policies. State agencies can foster cohesion, for example, by sending clear, consistent, and coherent messages to all districts (Lane and Gracia, 2004). In recent years, most of these messages have focused on uniform standards and performance targets. State policymakers have access and reach that many local districts cannot ever hope to achieve, and states can therefore play a special role in facilitating networks and engaging external partners (Lane and Gracia, 2004; Unger et al., 2008). For small to midsize districts, states play a critical role in pooling resources to achieve economies of scale (Unger et al., 2008).

States' power in education matters has grown in the past 50 years. Before the 1950s, states tended to play a minimal role in education, preferring to leave most control to local districts. The state role started to increase after the landmark *Brown v. Board of Education* case (1954), when states were required to assume the responsibility of ensuring equity for students. The federal government's role in education also grew, and state education agencies had to keep up to manage federal programs and ensure that districts and schools were complying with the rules and regulations that accompanied federal aid (Lane and Gracia, 2004; Fuhrman, Goertz, and Weinbaum, 2007). The state role increased even further after the publication of *A Nation at Risk* in 1983 and the subsequent reform movements of the 1980s and 1990s. The state share of education funding increased to 50 percent, legislatures became more professionalized, governors developed their own policy shops, and the business community began to get involved in education (Fuhrman, Goertz, and Weinbaum, 2007).

The state role increased again with the passage of the landmark No Child Left Behind Act of 2001. Before NCLB, states were primarily responsible for monitoring district behavior and ensuring compliance with federal and state regulations, particularly those related to categorical programs and special funding streams. With the advent of standards-based accountability and NCLB, states had to shift their focus to supporting districts and providing resources for school improvement. This is a new role that is outside most states' core competencies. Moreover, many state agencies have limited capacity, a problem that has been exacerbated by recent budget crises. These conditions make it challenging for states to adapt to interacting with districts and schools in a new way. Indeed, many of the strategies adopted by sites to build CLSs focus on building better relationships between state agencies and districts, as well as on developing ways to incentivize districts to change while also providing them with technical assistance to support the change process.

Strategies Pursued to Develop Cohesive Leadership Systems

We identified eight strategies commonly used to build CLSs. Most of them were adopted by states, with the exception of Kentucky, where the state and JCPS were equal partners in this work. Districts were, however, involved in implementing the strategies, mainly through their participation in state-created committees, consortia, and networks, or in joint PD experiences, such as the executive leadership programs with state leaders (at Harvard and the University of Virginia).

Many of these strategies overlapped and reinforced one another. For example, good communication sometimes fostered trust, and trust sometimes enhanced the strength of networks. Therefore, the strategies should not be considered distinct from one another.

Building Trust

Several interviewees described their efforts to build trust between the state and associated districts. This endeavor was reportedly necessary because several districts and states had monitoring and compliance relationships and had not previously worked as partners.

One approach used to build trust was explicitly acknowledging that improving leadership (and education in general) is both a state and a district responsibility. As an interviewee in Massachusetts stressed, "We are grappling with problems together . . . it's a district problem and a state problem, and no one has the answer to these problems."

Interviewees also described the importance of building trust by providing more support to districts, which in some cases meant deemphasizing states' monitoring function. Interviewees in Massachusetts noted that as the state increasingly worked with districts in collaborative ways—including listening to and then validating and addressing their concerns—it built credibility for the SEA and encouraged districts to collaborate with it. According to one SEA staff member, "Our face has grown friendly." An interviewee in Springfield (MA) concurred, stating, "It was like having inside help . . . the state was becoming a real partner in our work and not an adversary or just a compliance organization." In Georgia, interviewees reported that the new CSSO had enabled relationship-building between APS and the state and had contributed to better cooperation. An interviewee in Portland commented on this as well, stating, "I don't feel the 'gotcha' energy coming from [the SEA] anymore."

For some of the sites, trust-building was facilitated by attending executive leadership development programs, often with support from The Wallace Foundation. A team of Kentucky Department of Education representatives and leaders from four districts participated in Harvard's ExEL program, for example. The participating members from the Department of Education have continued to meet periodically to collaborate on instructional improvement. Interviewees who worked in the Department of Education noted that participation in ExEL encouraged collaboration among departments that had traditionally been quite isolated from one another. Similarly, Massachusetts interviewees noted that participation in the same ExEL program served as a venue in which the Massachusetts Department of Education and four district leaders coalesced as a professional learning community. Through this trust-building initiative, the state and the districts have improved their understanding of each other's positions and of how the state can better support the districts.

Creating Formal and Informal Networks

The majority of the sites created formal and informal networks as mechanisms for engaging stakeholders, building agreement among them, and developing policies and initiatives to improve school leadership. Networks also served as vehicles for dispersing information throughout the state as members communicated with others in their own local communities.

The most common approach to building formal networks across the sites was creating interagency coalitions, task forces, and committees with state and district representatives. In several sites, this approach was required by the Wallace Foundation grant. In response to Wallace requirements, the Iowa state association overseeing the work convened a broad stakeholder group, the Leadership Partnership, which met quarterly to develop cohesive policies and initiatives to support school leaders. Some states, including Kentucky, cemented such coalitions in legislation.

Coalitions brought together organizational representatives who did not routinely communicate. For example, in Kentucky, the Superintendents' CEO Network was established to advise the commissioner of education and provide PD for superintendents in the state. Members were selected from among superintendents of high-performing districts. Interviewees noted that the Superintendents' CEO Network was "a wonderful effort to try to build a professional community among superintendents and also to encourage superintendents to create professional communities of principals in their districts."

Indeed, interviewees reported that recruiting members for coalitions can be a strategic exercise. Some in Delaware emphasized the importance of including coalition members who have the power to create policies and influence change, along with others who will implement the changes. Delaware interviewees also stressed the importance of attracting "nay-sayers" to coalitions. Some sites, such as Kentucky, benefited from inviting external organizations to serve on coalitions as "critical friends." In Illinois, the involvement of teachers' unions helped ensure legislative support for the coalition's work. In Oregon, the SEA invited representatives of universities, professional associations, and district central offices to join OLN in an effort to gain broad-based buy-in for building much of the leadership improvement work around cultural competency. Members of Delaware's coalition included legislators and school board associations. In Indiana, the coalition included practicing principals and classroom teachers.

Sites faced challenges in structuring and timing participation. According to several interviewees in Massachusetts, not all stakeholders needed to be involved simultaneously in their coalition's work. In one stakeholder's words, "There needs to be different people at the table at different times. There should be continuity to ensure information sharing, but at different points you need different people." In Illinois, involving different people at different points in time did not work well. The original coalition approach was to establish small groups and work with them independently on separate issues (e.g., one group would work on licensure, while another focused on mentoring). However, this method built antagonism across members of the groups. The leadership of the CLS work in Illinois decided to bring all groups together at the same time in one large coalition that met four to five times a year, with smaller working groups focusing on specific issues.

Indeed, in many sites, coalitions were formed that represented actors from across the state, then smaller task forces or working committees were formed. Wallace funding and technical assistance helped Delaware to accelerate and deepen its leadership initiatives through its CLS coalition and the use of multiple task forces to share ideas, engage stakeholders, set priorities, and design and implement initiatives. Partnerships were formed in some sites to address specific topics. In Georgia, the Professional Standards Commission, GLISI, and the university system worked closely with SREB in the redesign of the principal pre-service preparation programs.

Sites also fostered informal networks as a means of building cohesion. As described above, informal networks sometimes grew from the experiences of state and district officials in the executive leadership development programs they attended. Sites also created informal networks through brokering relationships. For example, the grantee of record in Missouri was building relationships among individuals and programs, as noted by people at both state and district levels, including the St. Louis local educational agency. In particular, the grantee of record had pushed the local regional professional development center (RPDC) to work with St. Louis to deliver PD programs, overcoming both a culture of passivity ("the RPDCs lay out the goodies, the district takes what it wants") and a history of limited work with large urban districts.

Fostering Communications

A third strategy used in the sites to build cohesion was to foster regular communications among individuals and groups through meetings, e-mail, phone calls, and other means. Creating formal and informal networks facilitated this strategy, as did trust-building. Fostering communications was widespread, and interviewees at most of the sites stressed its importance. Ongoing communications often produced a common language, which should be useful in reaching agreement on how to improve school leadership across multiple individuals and organizations.

The most common way of communicating reported by the sites was holding regular meetings. The director of the Massachusetts CLS team reported that if three months passed without a meeting, "things began to fall apart." Meetings can be a vehicle for reiteration of vision. Such reiteration is important given that organizations have different agendas, and individuals have different perspectives. A Delaware interviewee stressed that "you have to continue to educate people about why this works and why it is important for the system to be collaborative."

Meetings are also forums for communicating new policies and providing updates on progress. In Indiana, the School Leaders Committee holds meetings around the state to communicate licensure changes and new requirements for preparation programs. In Delaware, an interviewee observed,

> [The CLS leader] will come to the state [board] at least two times a year. She'll give an overview and say this is where we are [in the CLS]. And then I went to something else a week later, I saw the overview again, maybe a month later. I said, I'm ready to give my support! That's where she does an excellent job [because] she makes sure everyone is kept informed, all of the stakeholders.

Interviewees reported that between meetings, leaders of these efforts dedicated time to calling and e-mailing others. The director of the Massachusetts CLS team reported that their work was enabled by team members talking and/or e-mailing every day. Whenever something came up that the director of the CLS work in Illinois thought others should know, she immediately started "working the phones." As one interviewee noted, "It takes many one-on-one conversations to move things." A lot of the work in Illinois was also done with e-mail; consortium members even used e-mail to draft and edit legislation text. In Delaware, Illinois, Kentucky, and Rhode Island, websites were used to keep track of and publish progress.

Another way sites fostered communication was by holding conferences or summits. A "leading for change" conference brought together members of the Kentucky Commonwealth Collaborative of School Leadership Programs, including all the universities that have principal preparation programs. This conference was followed by eight regional town hall meetings and a final statewide meeting involving a panel of national experts sharing their views on linking leadership to learning.

Communication has also been facilitated through focus groups. In Massachusetts, the state contracted with the University of Massachusetts to hold a series of focus groups with various district- and state-level stakeholders to elicit feedback on the draft revised standards. This approach facilitated communicating messages beyond coalition members.

Perhaps the most powerful communications took place when most of the key actors in a site could get together "in the same room," as our interviewees liked to say, to learn together and jointly decide on leadership improvements. Delaware was able to convene all its key actors fairly regularly by virtue of its small size. Iowa did so by its use of Wallace funds to subsidize travel costs to attend coordination and PD meetings. Kentucky got all its key stakeholders together sequentially through town hall meetings and monthly work group meetings.

Exerting Pressure and Influence

All the sites recognized that successful pursuit of their goals required buy-in at both the state and district levels, from both policymakers and practitioners. In addition to drawing on the strategies described above, they exerted pressure and influence to bring multiple stakeholders on board.

One way of exerting influence was to provide incentives (both rewards and sanctions) to induce action. In Massachusetts, state funding was an incentive for districts to provide instructional leadership in-service training. In Illinois, the state provided funding for mentoring programs. Other states awarded competitive pilot grants to ready and willing districts. Districts reported appreciation for these allocations, noting that they could then spend their own money on other efforts.

States also exerted pressure in the sites. In Illinois, the governor's office sent a letter to the Wallace-funded IL-SAELP consortium stipulating that it would support only recommendations for legislation that were made by a certain date. Kentucky pressured universities to reform their principal preparation programs. In Georgia and Iowa, all pre-service programs were subject to sunset provisions until it could be demonstrated that they were aligned with leadership standards and district needs.

States also exerted pressure by passing legislation or state board rules and regulations. Updating state board of education rules and regulations was often the path of least resistance for getting policies in place, although legislation was needed to fund new programs. Both are powerful mechanisms for requiring that programs and procedures be cohesive across districts and the state. District officials reported an appreciation for legislation not simply because it meant new funding for programs, but because it gave district officials an additional "excuse" to improve school leadership. Officials promoting initiatives could point to the state requirements as evidence of their necessity, without having to spend time and resources persuading others of their importance. Although legislation and regulations were generally seen as a major coup, some interviewees questioned whether programs would be implemented in accordance with the regulatory or legislative intent.

Promoting Improved Quality of Leadership Policies and Initiatives

The sites had a variety of mechanisms under way to improve the quality of leadership improvement initiatives and hold various organizations accountable for quality.

Several sites hired external experts as advisors when they were building their CLSs. Delaware's work was guided by several national leadership experts. Early in their work, Illinois CLS leaders asked SREB to ascertain how Illinois compared with SREB's member states in terms of progress on improving school leadership. Kentucky hired a nationally known expert on school leadership—and indeed, his presence at meetings incentivized participant attendance. Iowa offered additional training for mentors who wished to increase their skills beyond the one-day training provided to all mentors by contracting with the California-based New Teachers Center to provide their Coaching Leaders to Attain Student Success program. Delaware hired the New York Leadership Academy to train its coaches. Massachusetts convened a national expert panel prior to a Wallace convening to launch a conversation about the site's work. Goals of the panel included getting a national perspective on translating new leadership standards into components of preparation programs and evaluations to change leaders' practice; blocking out big pieces of the work (beginning with standards/licensure, evaluation, and program redesign); and determining the composition of an effective steering committee to champion and drive the CLS development process.

Another approach was to address district capacity constraints and provide resources, tools, and direct support to districts and schools. Iowa launched an initiative called Central Office Redesign, in which the CLS provided resources to the eight cities in the Urban Education Network to hire national coaches and redesign the roles of central office staff to better support principals as instructional leaders. Some states identified successful district practices and worked to bring them to scale, demonstrating an ability to identify and spread innovation. They accomplished this by securing additional resources to expand programs, creating networks to share practices, and sharing best practices at statewide and national conferences.

A final approach to ensuring quality (and accountability) across the sites was to require periodic leader preparation program approval from national organizations, such as the National Council for the Accreditation of Teacher Education, the Educational Leadership Constituent Council, and the National Association of State Directors of Teacher Education, or state-designed approval processes, such as the one developed in Kentucky. In many sites, programs that did not meet standards could be discontinued.

Building Capacity for the Work

Project leaders recognized early on that building a CLS would require a lot of effort and attention. While it might be argued that the SEA is the obvious organization to oversee leadership improvement efforts because of its mission and authority, some sites concluded that the SEA lacked the resources to carry out this work.

To assess internal capacity, some sites considered whether staff would be able to think and work outside the boundaries that are in place in many SEAs, which are typically organized around categorical federal programs (Wirt and Kirst, 1997; Unger et al., 2008). Some site actors also considered whether the SEA would be the most credible lead agency given the nature of the policies, initiatives, and changes under consideration. In some sites, the grantee of record was the SEA, but contracts were provided to professional associations and other organizations to carry out the work. This gave the leadership improvement initiatives the support of the state, along with the credibility of another organization to move the work forward.

Identifying Strong Individuals with Political and Social Capital to Lead the Work

Some sites moved their leadership agenda forward by nominating a director with high social and political capital who could work from an organizational base of appropriate power to exert pressure and influence. Interviewees in a few sites questioned whether directors of the leadership improvement work had strong power bases. In other sites, strong project directors had the reputation of having been successful instructional leaders themselves and/or of having a deep understanding of the role of an instructional leader. Strong directors also had political savvy and were capable facilitators of system change.

Connecting with Other Reform Efforts

Some sites were able to connect school leadership work with broader educational reform efforts in the state. Making such connections is a promising approach to supporting alignment and sustainability, but it requires a skilled and visionary coordinator or coordinating agencies that are sufficiently connected with other state leaders to ensure awareness of broader reform efforts. Connecting with other reforms can broaden the goal of cohesion from a focus only on leadership improvement policies and initiatives to building cohesion across multiple statewide education reform efforts. Building broad cohesion across a state may reduce the extent to which competing reform efforts threaten the viability of school leadership improvement work.

In Delaware, when a significant number of middle and high schools did not make adequate yearly progress (AYP) in 2004, leadership efforts were linked to an SEA agenda focused on improving achievement. The state targeted low-performing middle and high schools to participate in CLS initiatives.

In Kentucky, state leaders recognized that integrating leadership reform with other reform efforts could generate additional resources. They made the connection between their leadership work and existing initiatives to improve the quality of teachers and, by doing so, not only increased funding streams, but also sharpened the focus on the role of principals in supporting instructional improvement in their schools.

Differences in Strategies Across Sites

A natural question flowing from this description of key strategies is whether Delaware, Iowa, and Kentucky drew on some of these strategies more than others or pursued different approaches to achieving their goals. This section describes the main differences in strategies between these three sites and the others in our study.

Employing a Broad Range of Approaches with Wider Reach

Delaware, Iowa, and Kentucky pursued all eight strategies, while the other sites generally used fewer of them. In particular, these three sites were more likely to build capacity, identify strong individuals to lead the work, and connect the leadership work to other reform efforts than were the other sites.

Delaware, Iowa, and Kentucky all worked to build local capacity for leadership development and school improvement. Non-CLS sites—including Indiana, Missouri, Oregon, and Rhode Island—were less likely to build capacity by creating new state infrastructures. These sites, with the exception of Oregon, which did create a new structure, OLN, were more likely to support the leadership improvement agenda by housing their Wallace-funded projects within the SEA, staffed by existing personnel. They were less likely to create or enhance organizational capacity. Interviewees in these sites identified the limited capacity of the SEA as a barrier to the success of their leadership improvement agenda. In one site, leadership for the Wallace grant rotated among SEA staff, none of whom were allocated sufficient time for the work.

Respondents in Delaware, Iowa, and Kentucky were also more likely to have strong individuals with powerful social and political capital leading the work. Respondents in non-CLS sites were less likely to describe directors as having these characteristics. In one of the non-CLS sites, respondents described their leadership as "weak."

Finally, Delaware, Iowa, and Kentucky were more likely to connect their leadership improvement work to other reform efforts in their respective states. We found little evidence of connecting leadership work to other reform efforts in the non-CLS sites. Part of the reason may be that SEAs in those states are highly departmentalized, operating in what respondents often called "silos." Non-CLS site representatives also pointed to greater discord and mistrust between stakeholders and education agencies (and sometimes the governor), making it even more difficult to forge productive cross-agency and cross-department reform efforts. However, in general, these sites had few initiatives that were far enough along to connect to other reform efforts.

Strategic Communications

Leaders of the Wallace-funded work in Delaware and Iowa routinely gathered key state and district leaders into the same room to both learn about leadership and develop policies and initiatives to improve it. Kentucky accomplished this same goal in a serial fashion by traveling throughout the state, holding town hall meetings. Interviewees in these sites credited key state actors with creating "learning systems for leadership" to get to "leadership for learning." Routinely gathering key decisionmakers into one room enabled decisionmaking. Including those who would implement the decisions enabled buy-in.

Combining Pressure and Support

Another approach that differentiated Delaware, Iowa, and Kentucky from other sites in our sample was the employment of two key strategies simultaneously: exerting pressure for change and providing support for the change.

Kentucky's approach to redesigning its leader preparation programs is a prime example of the strength of this combination. The state agency governing educator preparation—the Education Professional Standards Board—publicly considered the possibility that it would change its regulations so that master's degrees would no longer be a prerequisite for candidates seeking principal preparation. This created pressure because higher education institutions immediately recognized that such a change could result in a major loss of enrollment in professional master's degree programs; thus they became motivated to get involved in the redesign efforts and have a say in the process.

But Kentucky did not rely on pressure alone; site leaders also offered support for the principal preparation program redesign process. The state and JCPS jointly hosted and organized a series of stakeholder forums, bringing in outside facilitators from highly regarded external organizations such as CCSSO, SREB, and the National Association of State Boards of Education. The CLS project provided funding for monthly two-day meetings of a working group that was composed primarily of representatives of higher education programs but also included representatives of key stakeholders such as the teachers' union and the Department of Education, as well as a highly regarded outside consultant. The state also launched a partnership with four universities to support the creation of a redesigned program, which provided an opportunity for evaluation and reflection on the elements of a high-quality program.

In non-CLS sites, pressure and support were less likely to be used together to drive a specific change agenda. One site changed its accreditation process for higher education programs by adopting more-rigorous program standards but did not provide support for attempts to redesign programs. Some stakeholders in the process were not optimistic that significant program change would occur. One participant speculated that programs would not invest the time to make meaningful change on their own, opting instead for superficial changes to meet the requirements.

These dual roles may be difficult to maintain. An interviewee in Iowa noted:

> Long-term, the area education agencies are at risk because we are sending multiple messages to them. We say they are there for support, yet in another week we ask them to do an accreditation visit and say harsh things to those people you serve. I don't have an answer for that, but that relationship long-term could get very fragile.

And according to another interviewee:

> Well it's hard. Because here we are the bad guys and here we are the good guys all rolled into one. And it's tough. . . . And that's been a little bit of a nut to crack; because how do we develop a philosophy that says, "We're going to monitor you, but we're also going to help you?"

Contextual Factors Enabling and Inhibiting Efforts to Build a CLS

Across the sites, interviewees reported a range of factors that enabled or hindered efforts to execute their strategies for building a CLS, most of which were in place prior to receipt of the Wallace Foundation grant:

Enabling factors
- Common structures and policies
- A history of collaboration
- Strong preexisting social networks
- Participation of nontraditional actors
- Funding and technical assistance from The Wallace Foundation
- Political support
- Supportive, stable, and aligned superintendents and school boards

Inhibiting factors
- Limited resources
- Limited SEA capacity
- Turnover of key staff
- Too many organizations, too far apart
- A culture of independence
- Discord across organizations
- Reform overload.

Enabling Factors

Common structures and policies. Across the sites, common structures and policies formed a foundation for ensuring cohesion. In Iowa, the CSSO governs P–16 education, which permits her to align policies across the entire system. It allows her to address the principal preparation programs, whose reform is vitally important to the K–12 sector but is often resisted by universities, which are, in many states, governed under separate authority structures.

Even in sites where the P-16 system is not aligned under one governing body, interviewees reported that state policies affecting all districts facilitated cohesion. All of the states in our study have common academic standards and assessments for students. Many are moving toward common high school graduation requirements (and some are moving toward common exit exams). Such standard experiences for youth contribute to developing principal preparation programs that address all districts' needs. And developing statewide policies primes states and districts for working together on subsequent policy issues.

A history of collaboration. Similarly, a history of collaborative, collegial relationships across organizations facilitates cohesion. Oregon's progressive social policies resonated well with both Portland and Eugene, and we found very little contention between state policy and our study districts' goals and priorities. In Iowa, multiple interviewees noted that the legislature and the Iowa Department of Education had an excellent relationship. One state agency interviewee reported that his organization had such a good relationship with the legislature that "sometimes it's scary." Similarly, an interviewee in Delaware noted, "Delaware would have done some of this the 'SAELP way' [anyway] because Delaware is a collaborative state."

Strong preexisting social networks. Another facilitator of cohesion is strong social networks that result from the same people serving in different roles over time, as was reportedly common in Delaware. It was also common in Delaware for educators to serve simultaneously on multiple boards and commissions, helping to link the work of diverse initiatives. We noted overlapping participation on different boards in Kentucky as well. And in Illinois, a CLS staff member used to work at the Illinois State Board of Education and therefore brought the perspective of that agency to the CLS work.

Small states may have an advantage in building such social networks. As one interviewee put it, "I think that Delaware does a really good job because Delaware is so small, everybody knows everybody and that makes a big difference; culture is family-like." A Rhode Island interviewee said that she "works directly with the Commissioner and Deputy Commissioner; it's so small in this state that you work with people directly." However, other interviewees in Rhode Island argued that although its small size has resulted in great familiarity among people and organizations, it has not facilitated collaboration among state government organizations.

Participation of nontraditional actors. Across the sites, several interviewees attributed progress in building cohesion to the involvement of actors other than SEAs. Interviewees credited professional associations, universities, state leadership academies, area education agencies, and "lead learner" districts with being as important as SEAs.

The Wallace Foundation. Not surprisingly, an important enabler for building cohesion in the sites was the funding, vision, and support of The Wallace Foundation. The Foundation has provided an unusual amount of nonmonetary support to grantees, such as opportunities to learn from each other through national interest groups, a website for grantees, occasional webinars, and regular grantee conferences.

Many interviewees noted that the grant brought disparate groups together. An interviewee in Massachusetts reported that Wallace

> got us to stop thinking so silo-like and start thinking more globally. . . . to bring all the players to the table for a reason and then to see some results.

Kentucky interviewees reported that prior to the Wallace work, stakeholders worked in isolation with their own individual agendas. A state agency interviewee there credited the Wallace grant and the leadership of the grantees with bringing stakeholders together around a common vision. According to an interviewee in Boston, the district and the state were partners "on paper" prior to 2006, but in response to prompting by Wallace, they began a more earnest and meaningful collaboration. She reported that in responding to the Wallace call for proposals, the leads from the SEA, Boston, and Springfield put forth a genuine effort to work together. A Delaware interviewee noted that the Wallace grant and resulting consortium encouraged CLS leaders to include universities in their leader development work.

Political support. Respondents noted that they were not the only ones committed to improving student achievement by improving school leadership and building a cohesive statewide system to do so; powerful state actors and organizations shared that commitment. A state-level interviewee in Kentucky noted that school leadership was at the top of the secretary of education's agenda.

Supportive, stable, and aligned superintendents and school boards. Interviewees reported both the stability and importance of supportive superintendents and board members in enabling districts to actively participate in building a CLS. Many also noted that superintendents and board members needed to be aligned in their vision to improve school leadership.

Inhibiting Factors

In addition to describing enablers, site representatives reported several challenges to building a CLS, some of which have existed for years. Others (such as turnover of key leaders) arose during efforts to build CLSs. Some of the barriers are nearly impossible to address, while others have been tackled in fairly creative ways. None of them were mentioned in all sites. One barrier may have prevented efforts from succeeding in one site, while other sites either did not face the same barrier or were able to overcome it.

Limited resources. Some interviewees reported that they lacked resources to build cohesive systems. Most interviewee complaints were about either a lack of time or a lack of staff. It is possible that we did not hear concerns about funding because these sites had all received Wallace grants. However, some of our study states were facing economic downturns and were experiencing education budget cuts, in some cases several percentage points a year, resulting in resource-strapped systems.

Limited SEA capacity. Some of the SEAs in our study also had limited capacity, both in numbers of staff and in staff with the knowledge and skills to lead the work. An interviewee in Providence noted that "RIDE [Rhode Island Department of Education] is extremely underresourced and lacking in capacity." Some respondents attributed limited capacity to resource issues such as declining state education budgets. Respondents in other sites attributed downsizing to a political desire for a lean state agency. Some interviewees reported that their SEAs were focused on helping rural districts and did not understand the complexity of the issues facing large urban districts in the state. Even in some sites that were actively working to build a CLS, respondents noted that SEA staff were "overworked and underpaid," resulting in limited capacity to support leadership development initiatives. Other interviewees, including some from Boston, however, reported that their SAEs did have the capacity to lead leadership improvement efforts.

Turnover of key staff. Several respondents noted that lack of continuity impeded creation of a CLS. Indiana was on its fourth SAELP leader since 2000, which may have contributed to limiting its accomplishments. Another non-CLS district had had four superintendents and five chief academic officers over the lifetime of the Wallace grant.

Too many organizations, too far apart. It may also be difficult to maintain cohesion when organizations are highly dispersed. Springfield (MA) is a two-hour drive from Boston, and the state SEA is located in Malden, which made it difficult to arrange in-person meetings between Boston, Springfield, and SEA representatives. The large number of higher education preparation programs in Massachusetts also hindered cohesion. Since there was no easy way to involve all 35 of the preparation providers in the working group that was creating the standards, none were directly involved in decisionmaking[1] (except the University of Massachusetts–Amherst, which conducted some background work under a contract).

Culture of independence. In addition to geographic constraints, structures and cultures that promote independence can constrain cohesion (although they may have benefits as well). One non-CLS site's interviewees noted the state's history of local control and independence; another interviewee remarked that the state's "mascot" was the "Independence Man," a lone figure that stands on top of the state capitol building. Similarly, in Oregon, the political culture of education promotes and supports local control. Top-down state-level initiatives have generally not been enthusiastically embraced there.

Discord among organizations. In some sites, there is fragmentation among and between state organizations and districts. Numerous interviewees in one site noted that their state legislature is not a reliable partner in education improvement because it often "goes off on its own" and passes legislation that is "not helpful to anyone." Interviewees in another site reported that the superintendent of schools had advised teachers not to take their students to the state capital for a traditional field trip, but to take them instead to a neighboring state, where "state government works." In one non-CLS site, the state legislature cut funds to the SEA because of what it perceived to be the SEA's poor handling of the deaccreditation of a large urban district.

Interviewees in Kentucky reported that the Wallace funding and technical assistance had been instrumental in overcoming discord between Jefferson County and the SEA and facilitating joint work. Requiring the district and the state to sit down together and negotiate the budget and other tasks in the grant resolved their differences and aligned their expectations of each other.

Reform overload and other external threats. Districts in particular complained that they were struggling to balance several externally imposed initiatives. Even those that were committed to improving school leadership were also implementing other programs to improve student achievement—for example, by focusing on English-language learners. Interviewees reported struggling to ensure that their reform efforts were aligned across many different areas as they attempted to mirror the cohesion around leadership improvement policies and initiatives that was building in their states.

Contextual Differences Across Sites

Delaware and Iowa had a history of collaboration and strong social networks. They also, along with Kentucky, had a history of political support for school reform.

---

[1] During the vetting process, the standards were reviewed by an organization that represents three associations of higher education.

Delaware and Iowa have both had relatively positive relationships among deeply networked state-level stakeholders and a history of collaboration among them. We noted overlapping participation on different boards in Kentucky as well, but interviewees noted that this site did not have a history of positive, collaborative relationships between state and district actors. Only with the advent of the Wallace funding and support had leaders from the SEA and Jefferson County been able to mend fences and begin to work collaboratively.

Delaware, Iowa, and Kentucky also reported a consistently high level of political support stemming from a widely shared vision for reform among political leaders. All three sites had a history of state activism in education reform. The shared experiences set the groundwork for progress on leadership initiatives by facilitating discussions on how to address educational leadership issues.

Finally, we examined whether the more advanced sites faced fewer serious barriers to cohesion. We found that Delaware, Iowa, and Kentucky were less likely to have had turnover of key staff, a culture of independence, and discord across organizations. However, these sites did have to overcome limited resources and SEA capacity, dispersed organizations, and, in the case of Kentucky, a history of tension between the SEA and the Jefferson County school district.

Conclusions

We conclude that state actors can be highly effective in developing cohesive leadership systems when they take deliberate action to build broad engagement and agreement across multiple, diverse stakeholders. Delaware, Iowa, and Kentucky achieved strong systems by implementing effective strategies. For example, these states created models of distributed leadership for the work, which included key roles for legislatures, CSSOs, SEAs, universities, professional associations, and key district leaders, as described in Chapter Four. They were also more likely than other states to

- Employ a broad range of other strategies, with a focus on identifying strong individuals to lead the work and connecting the leadership work to other reform efforts
- Prioritize strategic communications sessions in which multiple key stakeholders came together to develop leadership improvement policies and initiatives
- Use a combination of pressure and support to further their leadership agendas.

These three states also had a history of positive and collaborative relationships among stakeholders, political support, and a lower rate of staff turnover, factors that were not present in many of the other states.

In the sites with more-advanced CLSs, district respondents reported three types of benefits: more-sophisticated support, increased funding, and, in those states where specific improvement actions were mandated, an "excuse" to improve school leadership. Because the study districts reported benefits from state involvement, we suspect that smaller, less-resourced districts would also benefit from it.

Interviewees in sites with less-developed leadership systems reported very few examples of strategies that had failed. They attributed lack of progress to contextual barriers rather than strategic errors. The two most often cited contextual barriers were turnover of key staff and a culture of independence and local control over education policy.

In Chapter Nine, we will draw some practical lessons from our analysis for states that want to embark on creating CLSs.

CHAPTER SEVEN

Prospects for Sustainability

Interviewees from all 10 sites in our study talked about continuing the work they had begun. Some sites were planning to spread leadership improvement beyond pilot districts; others had accomplished much in one specific area, such as standards for leaders, and hoped to expand the work to other aspects of leadership, such as principal preparation programs. But most of our interviewees recognized that scaling up would be challenging—as would sustaining the progress they had made—after Foundation funding ends in 2010. In this chapter, we present lessons learned on ways to continue the work and address future funding challenges.

Challenges to Sustainment and Expansion

Most of our interviewees were hoping to sustain their work but were uncertain about whether they would be able to do so. Their main concerns were about resource constraints, staff turnover, ongoing organizational commitment, and loss of fidelity in implementation as new districts and schools came on board.

Interviewees were concerned about insufficient time or staff, as well as future funding. An interviewee in Massachusetts noted:

> In these early stages of laying the groundwork [for collaborating on the standards], it's been all about time. Because the more time we spend together, the better the work gets . . . but everyone is so busy.

Interviewees in Kentucky stated that they would like to oversee PD by ensuring that approved providers will focus on leadership practices to improve student achievement in their offerings to principals, but they lacked the staff to review all of the offerings. Others expressed concern about funding and suggested strategies to garner additional funds, described below.

Interviewees in Iowa were most worried about staff turnover. According to one respondent:

The difficult part when you try to project political will is that it's volatile, so changing. I anticipate we'll get a new director of DOE [the Iowa Department of Education] in the next few years, and the Executive Director of SAI [School Administrators of Iowa]—key leadership positions. There will be changing of the superintendencies in the UEN [Urban Education Network, which consists of eight large districts in Iowa]. There is a trend to bring in new people from out of state, people who don't have a deep understanding of the work. Will things remain a focus once these key leaders retire and move on? That will be the mark of whether or not it really truly took hold, if we built capacity. We have good leaders in Iowa and people who are committed to the work that is outlined in the Wallace work. It's a matter of what's next. It's hard to predict, hard to know what the system will become.

Another Iowa interviewee described the director of the current CLS program as "incredible" and worried about the fate of the initiative once she steps down:

Is this a sustainable future, or is it because this one person worked tirelessly and we had the wonderful funding from Wallace? It's worrisome to think when the critical pivot person is gone, then what?

A few interviewees expressed concern that some organizations had become involved because they needed funding for their own programs, not because they were committed to the larger goal of improving instructional leadership. In one case, respondents said that organizations that were offering training for mentors had lobbied hard to receive state funding but had not embraced the mentoring model many CLS participants had spent months honing. As the literature indicates and our research confirms, tension can exist between each partner's own distinct identity and the collective identity, between self-interest and the collective interest; the partners need to have "mutually beneficial interdependencies" to sustain the collaboration.

A related concern was that it would be difficult to stay faithful to the full intent of the initiative as new organizations came on board. In several states, scale-up hinges on further implementation of the work in local districts and schools. There is tension between building cohesion across state and district agencies and respecting local contexts in implementing CLSs. For example, Iowa now requires evaluations based on the state leadership standards. Principals are evaluated by superintendents, and their PD is based on the evaluation results. But it remains to be seen whether these evaluations will be taken seriously and conducted with fidelity to their intent. Many district interviewees argued that their district was different from others in their state (larger or smaller, more urban or more rural), so that future efforts would need to be further tailored. Districts may also differ by region. Respondents in Kentucky noted that "state culture varies a lot by region (e.g., eastern versus western Kentucky), so it can be difficult to agree on a common vision." Similarly, leadership efforts in Oregon have focused primarily on the more progressive and urban western part of the state. Tension between broad reforms and local implementation is certainly not unique to building a CLS, but it is worth considering in this context.

Strategies for Sustainment and Growth

We asked our interviewees how the sites were planning to address the challenges to sustaining and expanding their systems. Many were convinced that the most effective strategy was to legislate and regulate initiatives. In several states, including Delaware, Illinois, Iowa, Kentucky, and Massachusetts, interviewees prided themselves on passing legislation and promulgating regulations supporting the CLS work.

Existing legislation has provided stable funding for some initiatives. An interviewee in Massachusetts noted, "I'm getting lots of other funding from the legislature itself, which says, 'Gosh, this is great. This Wallace Foundation has funded it, but we've got to be able to support it too.'" In Iowa, a legislator recommended collecting data to demonstrate that leadership is making a difference in student achievement as a strategy to continue to engage legislative bodies.

To shield efforts against turnover and transitions, sites were documenting their work, doing succession planning, establishing distributed leadership systems, and vesting leadership of efforts in apolitical organizations, such as universities, to enable programs to outlast political changes in departments of education. In Kentucky, the CLS project leader partnered with the Kentucky Leadership Academy as part of an explicit strategy to build sustainability. In Massachusetts, state actors have worked to establish distributed leadership and a collaboration in which multiple individuals from different organizations feel ownership and responsibility for the work.

Individual organizational interests have been balanced with the interests of improving school leadership across a state by creating incentives for ongoing participation in CLS efforts; demonstrating the importance of this work through research and early successes; and developing and maintaining common understandings, shared goals, and joint ownership. Achieving "early wins" has helped individual organizations recognize benefits from engaging in CLS work. Delaware used mini-grants to seed practices (e.g., succession planning, distributed leadership) in high-functioning pilot districts and then publicized their work, hoping that the pilots would serve as models. As a Delaware interviewee noted:

> We got a lot of things to happen right up front so skeptics were able to see tangible change quickly, so some skeptics bought into the system, they saw results. And they [results] have continued to happen.

To maintain fidelity as new organizations, particularly new districts and schools, take on the CLS work, states have provided PD and technical assistance. Some sites developed products and technologies that would outlast the initiators of the work.

Finally, as described above, state actors have aligned their work with leadership standards in the hope that new organizations will understand that referent point and, even if they adjust programs and procedures to meet local needs, will maintain the alignment.

Many respondents expressed the belief that achieving a certain level of cohesion through the concerted efforts of state and district leaders was in itself a hedge against dissolution in the future. Several commented that there was no turning back: Bonds had been formed, a common language and vision had been embraced, and widespread commitment to mutual goals had developed. In other words, the groundwork had been laid, and momentum had been gained. State officials in several sites noted that they had established collaborative norms and routines. A Portland interviewee said, "It is not going to go away. We don't want this to die." A member of the Oregon Professors of Educational Administration argued that this organization "will remain because we have now recognized through our cooperation that we are stronger together." In Kentucky, a state leader stressed that he is committed to "staying around to see the redesign work through." In the words of one Massachusetts interviewee:

> I think the collaboration is not an option anymore. . . . I think that the leadership alliance [collaboration of professional associations, service providers, and the SEA] is institutionalized. . . . we came together because of a grant, but now, we're there because of the concept and the ideas and the vision we have. You know, they helped us create a vision for what we needed to do. So, while we had the money—the Wallace grant, at first, was important. If we lost Wallace dollars today, the leadership alliance would still be meeting, would still be working together. That's exciting.

Conclusions

These responses suggest that sites that are the furthest along in developing a CLS are likely to sustain the work and build upon it in the future. Leaders in these sites have been using creative strategies to overcome difficulties—formalizing their efforts in a legislated policy framework, garnering additional resources, distributing leadership roles, and demonstrating early wins—and they have expressed high levels of commitment. Indeed, the structural and process components of building a CLS both appear to be important factors in sustaining the work. Interviewees in sites that have strong alignment across policies and initiatives at the state and district level are hopeful that the investments they have made in alignment will help ensure that future policies and initiatives are also aligned to state standards and to each other. Finally, in sites where collaborative routines and behaviors had become the norm, interviewees predicted that states and districts will continue their joint work to improve school leadership.

CHAPTER EIGHT

Support for the CLS Hypothesis

In this chapter, we examine the assumptions behind the CLS hypothesis. Up to this point, we have analyzed the sites' CLS-building efforts with the help of Foundation funding and technical support. We now ask whether these efforts are likely to reap the benefits they were designed to achieve: improved school leadership that supports improved student learning. We did not set out to examine effects on student learning, but we did examine whether the sites that had achieved the most-advanced leadership systems could be associated with other positive outcomes. In the following, we describe the research evidence that would indicate an association between cohesive policies and certain benefits, then we describe whether we found any such evidence.

The Wallace Foundation hypothesized that if states and districts work together to improve leadership standards, training for leaders, and the conditions leaders face, school leaders can be more effective. We attempted to examine these connections in our principal surveys and found that it was difficult to analyze principals' training and leadership standards, because their years of experience varied and they had completed many different preparation programs. Furthermore, although many were aware that their states had leadership standards, they could not identify a direct connection between those standards and other leadership improvement policies or initiatives.

However, principals provided a good deal of useful information on their conditions. With those data, we were able to describe specific conditions facing principals, including the extent to which they perceived they had the data, autonomy, resources, and accountability systems they required to be effective. We also asked principals whether they engaged in certain leadership practices, such as developing and implementing strategic goals and supporting the instruction of students, practices that studies have associated with improved student achievement. We then assessed whether principals who reported better conditions were more likely to engage in those practices. We also examined whether the responses of principals in the CLS sites differed from those of principals in the non-CLS sites.

Demonstrating a relationship between better conditions and more time on instructional leadership is not sufficient to demonstrate that one causes the other, since other factors may be influencing these outcomes. Nor does it offer any insight into whether greater cohesion improves either conditions or engagement in leadership practices. Nevertheless, demonstrating a positive association between positive conditions and greater engagement in instructional practices would offer some support for the Wallace hypothesis.

The CLS model defines effective school leaders as principals who (1) establish high expectations for all students, (2) use data and other means to diagnose shortfalls in instructional effectiveness and implement plans to strengthen instruction, and (3) focus attention and resources on improving instruction (The Wallace Foundation, 2006). A number of studies have indicated the importance of practices such as setting a vision or schoolwide goals, creating new learning opportunities for students and staff, directly observing classroom practices and providing quality feedback, promoting discussion about instructional issues, emphasizing the use of test results for program improvement, and developing opportunities for staff to participate in leadership (see, for example, Elmore, 2000; Fink and Resnick, 2001; Blase and Blase, 2004; Leithwood et al., 2004; The Wallace Foundation, 2006). In particular, observing classroom practices and providing quality feedback to teachers are considered central to learning-centered leadership (NCSL, 2007).

Recent studies have found that most principals do not spend as much time on activities directly related to learning as they would like. In a study on the implementation of SAMs in Jefferson County, most principals reported spending about 30 percent of their time on learning-centered activities prior to working with a SAM (Holland, 2008). More than two-thirds of the principals surveyed in a study in Pittsburgh were dissatisfied with the amount of time they were able to spend observing in classrooms and wanted to spend less time on administrative activities, such as dealing with budget, personnel, and administrative paperwork (Tharp-Taylor et al., 2009).

The CLS model assumes that the following critical conditions are particularly important: (1) adequate data to inform principals' decisions, (2) enough autonomy to enable them to direct resources (human and financial) where they are needed, and (3) supportive and transparent PD, evaluation, and accountability systems. This, too, is supported by research, which suggests that school leaders can be more effective if they have positive conditions (IEL, 2000; Portin et al., 2003; Leithwood et al., 2004; Knapp et al., 2006).

Our survey of principals was designed to provide data we could analyze to discover whether there is a link between positive conditions and more engagement in the reportedly effective leadership practices. It is important to note that our survey data were self-reported, and responses were therefore subjective. Even so, the survey responses provided an understanding of what principals consider to be enablers and hindrances in their working environments. We asked principals about the nature of the data they had available; the resources they had at their disposal; evaluations and PD; and their decisionmaking authority and autonomy. We also asked them whether governing agencies' roles and responsibilities were aligned; whether the policies under which they worked were burdensome, conflicting, or fragmented; whether they had assistance with administrative duties; and whether their administrative staff was sufficient in number and of high quality.

To learn about their instructional leadership practices, we asked principals to report the time and effort they had spent on instructional leadership practices during the prior school year and whether the time spent was appropriate or sufficient. The practices included (1) developing and implementing strategic goals and school improvement efforts, (2) supporting the instruction of students, and (3) promoting the development and leadership of the school's teachers and staff. (Details of the construction of the indices for conditions and instructional leadership practices are provided in Appendix E.) We supplemented our analyses with interview and log data to highlight insights we gained from principals.

We present our survey findings in three sections. We first examine principals' conditions, focusing on principals in CLS sites, because the Foundation determined that progress had been made on improving conditions in these sites. We then turn to principals' reports on instructional leadership, again focusing on the CLS sites. We compare survey results from the CLS principals with those from the non-CLS principals to see whether there are differences between their perspectives on either conditions or instructional leadership practices by comparing mean differences between the survey responses of principals in the CLS sites (Delaware, Georgia, Illinois, Iowa, Kentucky, and Massachusetts) and those in the non-CLS sites (Indiana, Missouri, Oregon, and Rhode Island). Because we did not find many significant differences between the principals in these two groups, we grouped all of our survey respondents together and analyzed the relationship between conditions principals face and the time they spend on instructional leadership, the main focus this chapter. We conducted regression analyses to control for school characteristics and principal tenure to isolate relationships between reported conditions and leadership practices across all sites. We report standardized coefficients to indicate the magnitude of these relationships.[1] (Details of our methodological approach and analyses are presented in Appendix F.)

Conditions

Responses of principals in CLS sites on their conditions were neither overwhelmingly positive nor negative (Figure 8.1).[2]

---

[1] A standardized coefficient is created by setting the means of all the variables in the model to 0, with a standard deviation of 1. A coefficient of 1.0 indicates that an increase of 1 standard deviation in a condition will bring about a 1-standard-deviation increase in the instructional leadership practice.

[2] Principals' responses varied greatly within the same district. The differences in perceptions could be due to different levels of expectations about the conditions, or they could signal a difference in principals' satisfaction with the district support or leadership. We were unable to probe further into the reasons for differences among principals' perceptions within each district using our survey data.

Figure 8.1
Mean Responses of Conditions for Principals in CLS Sites

	Strongly disagree 0	Disagree 1	Agree 2	Strongly agree 3
1. Receive quality data (N=340)			1.8	
2. Receive sufficient resources (N=338)		1.4		

	Not at all 0	To a small extent 1	To a moderate extent 2	To a large extent 3
3. Have aligned governance (N=328)			2.0	
4. Politics are burdensome, conflicting, and fragmented (N=332)		1.5		
5. Receive quality district-provided tools, PD, and evaluations (N=336)			1.9	
6. District provides administrative support (e.g., school administration manager (SAM)) (N=336)	0.9			
7. District provides quality and sufficient leadership staff in school (N=333)		1.4		

	None 0	Some 1	A lot 2	Complete 3
8. Authority (N=337)		1.7		

RAND *MG885-8.1*

Data. Most principals were satisfied with the data they had at their disposal from the state and the district. On average, principals in the CLS sites agreed that the student assessment data they received were organized and easily accessible, accurate and reliable, and useful for helping staff improve teaching and learning (mean = 1.8). However, when we looked specifically at the extent to which state data were timely (presented in Table F.2), the CLS principals were, on average, dissatisfied with data timeliness (mean = 1.0).

Resources. On average, principals disagreed that they had sufficient resources (mean = 1.4), i.e., time, money, and personnel. This index comprises questions about the extent to which states and districts allocate resources fairly; the principal's access to sufficient resources to meet the academic, emotional, and social needs of students; the adequacy of facilities and transportation; and the adequacy of time and staff for the principal to effectively lead the school. Principals' responses to these questions were not surprising given that in other research, principals often noted a lack of resources as a key constraint on their effectiveness (e.g., Johnson, Arumi, and Ott, 2006). Studies also suggest that the increased emphasis on the principal's responsibility for instructional leadership has not brought about a concomitant decrease in administrative duties (Lashway, 2002; Marks and Printy, 2003).

Aligned governance and burdensome/conflicting policies. On average, principals in CLS sites reported that the roles and responsibilities of governing entities were moderately aligned (mean = 2.0) and that state and district policies were burdensome, conflicting, or fragmented to a small to moderate extent (mean = 1.5).

Quality tools, PD, evaluations, and other administrative staff. Principals in CLS sites reported that their districts provided tools and training on data, high-quality PD opportunities, and performance evaluations that were based on state leadership standards, were focused on instructional leadership, and were clear and transparent to a moderate extent (mean = 1.9). They reported that their district provided direct assistance with administrative duties to only a small extent (mean = 0.9). Similarly, they reported that their district provided sufficient and qualified leadership staff (e.g., assistant principals or school-based coaches) to a small extent (mean = 1.4).

Authority. On average, principals in CLS sites reported having between some and a lot of authority over a number of schooling decisions (mean = 1.7). However, some clear differences emerged on specific items (see Table F.9 in Appendix F). Principals in CLS sites reported having a lot of authority over hiring teachers (mean = 2.2), setting the school's schedule (mean = 2.2), and setting achievement goals (mean = 1.9). They reported having only some authority over evaluating teachers (mean = 1.2), removing teachers (mean = 1.4), and removing administrators (mean = 1.2).

Principals in non-CLS sites reported a lower level of authority, on average (mean = 1.2). As shown in Table F.9, principals in CLS sites reported having significantly more authority over establishing the school's curriculum, selecting textbooks, and removing teachers than principals in non-CLS sites had. This may be a result of the efforts made in the CLS sites to improve conditions, or it may simply be due to variance in the districts studied that is not related to CLS-building efforts. Our interviews with district personnel did not provide a consensus on what would constitute ideal authority levels across schools in their districts; indeed, reports on this topic were conflicting.

Principals themselves held different views on the value of autonomy. In the open-ended survey responses, some principals reported that they appreciated having the district provide them with research-based curricula and associated textbooks. In interviews, some principals praised the district for providing standardized curricula across all schools, because it facilitated mobile students' success. But others would have preferred more control over the curriculum. In some cases, the desire for control seemed to be related to a desire to satisfy teachers who wanted to keep a curriculum they knew and liked. One principal reported that "teachers resent a new literacy curriculum. Our school's version is excellent. I advised teachers to integrate good parts of the new one and keep the old one."

In the interviews, many more principals noted their lack of authority over removing teachers and administrators (often referencing unions as an obstacle) than their lack of authority over the curriculum. They wanted to be able to remove poorly performing teachers, although it appeared that they would not remove many: 65 percent of surveyed principals would remove only 1 to 10 percent of their teachers, if they could, and another 22 percent would remove 11 to 25 percent. This finding aligns with the findings of recent research in California. When asked what change would help them improve student outcomes most, principals most often cited greater freedom to fire teachers. This authority was more important to them than additional resources of any variety (Fuller et al., 2007).

While there is little empirical evidence to suggest that granting principals more authority over hiring or firing decisions would lead to improved student learning, most of the principals in our study considered lack of such authority to be an important barrier to doing their job effectively. Principals we interviewed reported spending much time and energy on multiple year-long removal processes for a small number of teachers. Because this process takes time and attention, students are subjected to poor teaching in the meantime, and principals are prevented from spending time on other efforts to improve instruction. One principal said, "I have some teachers who are not getting the job done. Putting them on an improvement plan is a two- or three-year process which means 600 kids are flushed away." Another survey respondent wrote:

> Until I have the authority to hire the right teachers and to remove those who are underperforming, there will be relatively few changes in true academic growth of students. The teachers' union has more control of outcomes than administration—that doesn't seem right.

In sum, principals in CLS sites reported, on average, that state and district data were organized, reliable, and useful, but that state data were not timely. They also reported that they did not have sufficient resources, on average (funding, time, or staff). Governing bodies appeared to be moderately aligned, and districts seemed to be providing principals with quality PD, evaluations, and other tools. Yet principals reported insufficient administrative support or additional leadership staff, such as assistant principals and coaches. Furthermore, principals in CLS sites reported having a lot of autonomy over some schooling decisions but expressed a desire for more authority to remove teachers who performed poorly.

Instructional Leadership Practices

Table 8.1 shows the mean responses for time spent and appropriateness of time spent on instructional leadership practices of principals in CLS sites. On average, principals spent time on a variety of instructional leadership practices and reported that the time they spent was appropriate.[3]

---

[3] We found some variation at the school level (not shown). Primary school principals reported spending more time on school improvement, motivating students, engaging teachers, and promoting staff PD than principals of middle and high schools did. They also reported being more satisfied with the time they spent building a common

Table 8.1
CLS Principals' Responses on Time Spent and Appropriateness of Time Spent on Instructional Leadership Practices

Practice	Time Spent[a] (mean)	Appropriateness[b] (mean)
Development and implementation of strategic goals and school improvement efforts		
Building a common vision (N = 326)	0.47	0.68
School improvement efforts (N = 326)	0.64	0.77
Supporting the instruction of students		
Ensuring a supportive learning environment (N = 327)	0.75	0.77
Motivating students (N = 327)	0.58	0.76
Monitoring classroom instruction (N = 325)	0.30	0.58
Engaging with teachers outside of the classroom (N = 327)	0.58	0.74
Promoting the development and leadership of the school's teachers and staff		
Promoting staff professional development (N = 326)	0.46	0.71
Motivating staff (N = 325)	0.44	0.72
Developing leadership teams (N = 325)	0.55	0.79

[a] Scale: 0 = no time or some time and effort; 1 = a great deal of time and effort.
[b] Scale: 0 = insufficient or excessive for this school; 1 = appropriate and sufficient.

Principals generally reported spending most of their time and effort on practices related to ensuring that the school provided a supportive environment for student learning (mean = 0.75). This index comprises survey questions related to ensuring that disruptions of instructional time are minimized and the establishment of a safe and orderly environment.

On average, principals in CLS sites reported spending the least time and effort on tasks related to monitoring classroom instruction (mean = 0.30). They were also least likely to report that the time spent on this practice was sufficient (mean = 0.58). This index included such activities as collecting and examining student work, organizing walkthroughs or classroom visits, and reviewing and providing feedback on teacher lesson plans.

Comments in the end-of-day logs and interviews illustrate principals' frustration with the lack of time spent in the classroom. One principal noted in an interview that much of her time was spent on complying with district mandates, rather than on educating students. She noted that "more time [is] spent on chasing paperwork rather

---

vision, creating a supportive environment for students, engaging teachers, motivating staff, and fostering leadership among their staff.

than ensuring that teachers are teaching these kids." Another principal noted in her end-of-day log that repeated interruptions throughout the day interfered with the time she could have devoted to visiting classes:

> I planned to conduct a series of walkthroughs but was hindered by having to respond to situations that arose all day. I was hindered by still not having an assistant or an experienced secretary or additional support staff so that I had to take care of the behavior issues, parent concerns, personnel issues, purchasing issues, etc., that were more than in a normal day. By the time these things were taken care of, there was no time to do my walkthroughs. I will try again tomorrow.

A principal in a different district also noted the difficulty of finding time to get into the classroom. In one end-of-day log, she commented:

> [Attending to instructional leadership] is what I worry about the most and [what] keeps me up at night. The other stuff can completely take over your life. [I have] 26 initiatives going on in my building. I am grateful to have parents who manage most of those initiatives with me, but if I let it take over my day I would never be able to see that classroom.

We examined differences between mean responses of principals in CLS sites and those in non-CLS sites on all of the instructional leadership practice indices. Findings are displayed in Tables F.10 through F.27 in Appendix F. On average, principals in non-CLS sites reported spending significantly less time on developing leadership teams than did principals in CLS sites (see Table F.26). This is the only practice of the nine we posed on the survey on which CLS principals' responses differed from those of non-CLS principals. We therefore found little evidence that CLS principals were able to spend more time on instructional leadership practices. As described below, conditions such as authority, PD, and evaluation systems were related to time spent on instructional leadership practices. It could be that even though CLS sites were found to have made progress on improving conditions, districts had not fully developed PD or evaluation systems that supported and incentivized instructional leadership practices. Furthermore, we found a lack of consensus on principals' optimal levels of authority.

A more telling difference between the CLS and non-CLS principals was that the latter were significantly more likely to report spending insufficient time on most of the instructional leadership practices: school improvement efforts (Table F.13), creating a supportive learning environment for students (Table F.15), motivating students (Table F.17), engaging with teachers outside of the classroom to improve instruction (Table F.21), promoting staff development (Table F.23), and motivating staff (Table F.25). These findings suggest that principals in non-CLS sites were more dissatisfied with how they spent their time than were principals in the CLS sites. Our data did not allow us to speculate on why this might be the case.

Links Between Favorable Conditions and Engagement with Instructional Leadership Practices

We found that for nearly every condition, favorable reports were positively associated with more engagement in instructional leadership practices. (Only one condition did not show this correlation, as described below.) Furthermore, availability of adequate resources was positively related to engagement in (and appropriateness of time spent on) *all* instructional leadership practices. On their end-of-day logs, many principals reported that lack of adequate resources hindered their ability to engage in a particular practice on the day in question. This was the most frequently reported hindrance.

We also found the following links between conditions and practices:

- District-provided PD, tools, and evaluations had the strongest relationship with time spent on instructional leadership practices, particularly for monitoring classroom instruction and engaging with teachers outside of the classroom to improve instruction. In the interviews, many principals reported that the support of their supervisor and the PD they received were strong enablers of their ability to lead their schools.
- Timely access to reliable and useful data was positively related to time spent on a number of instructional leadership practices and principals' perceptions of the appropriateness of time spent. In particular, principals who reported having access to better data also reported spending more time on building a common vision and monitoring classroom instruction. Our qualitative data provided some examples of how principals used data to improve classroom instruction. One survey respondent wrote, "More focus on data-driven decisions has improved understanding of student progress. . . . It has sharpened and deepened the teacher's conversation about instruction and what constitutes good instruction."
- Authority over decisionmaking was positively related to time spent on almost all of the instructional leadership practices and was most correlated with principals' time spent on promoting staff PD and motivating staff. It also had a positive relationship with appropriateness of time spent building a common vision, monitoring classroom instruction, and developing leadership staff.

Interestingly, the one condition that was *not* linked to engagement in leadership practices was conflicting, burdensome, or fragmented policies. That is, the absence of this condition did not appear to improve time spent on instructional practices. Neither did this condition impede instructional leadership practices (i.e., we did not find a negative association between them). One possible explanation for this finding is that principals may have found ways to circumvent burdensome policies. For example, an elementary school principal with four years of experience told us in an interview, "I think outside the box and don't let the district stop me." An elementary school principal with three years of experience reported that "principals just have to do what's right and ask for permission later." A high school principal near retirement said that because he is at end of his career, he feels free to "act out." A high school principal reported hiring teachers who did not yet have tenure so she could fire them if necessary and that she had recently hired someone to serve as dean who was not qualified for this role according to district rules. Instead of confronting the district, she hired him under another title, with an agreement that he function as dean. (For detailed findings, see Tables F.28 through F.43.)

Conclusions

Overall, principals in CLS sites were somewhat discontented with their conditions, and their responses highlight areas for improvement. The CLS model emphasizes the importance of states working with districts to ensure that conditions such as levels of autonomy, targeted resources, and data are sufficient to enable effective school leadership. More work is needed on improving these conditions, with a particular focus on timely state data, authority levels, and sufficient resources.

Our survey findings, log reports, and interviews provide modest support for the CLS hypothesis by showing that perceptions of more-positive conditions were associated with principals spending more time on practices that have been linked to improved student learning. However, we recognize the limitations of this analysis: We could not confirm that these are causal relationships (it could be that leaders who have more time for instructional leadership are more satisfied with their work in general or that they are more generous in their assessment of their conditions), and we cannot establish a link between more-cohesive leadership systems and better conditions, or between more-cohesive systems and more engagement with effective practices. That would require further analysis of many more principals across the country, including those in districts that are not part of the Wallace network.

CHAPTER NINE

Recommendations

We have shown that it is possible to develop CLSs between states and districts to improve school leadership. We have identified the approaches that appear most effective in developing such systems, as well as certain local conditions that create a favorable environment for this work. Several of the sites in our study have achieved significant policy changes, particularly in principal preparation programs and statewide principal evaluation systems. State actors were most likely to be taking the lead in building CLSs, although districts played important roles and had many school leadership improvement initiatives under way. Many of our interviewees at both the state and district levels expressed high levels of engagement, enthusiasm, and dedication to their work in this area. They were optimistic that a more-cohesive leadership system would lead to better student outcomes and were putting strategies in place to sustain the progress they had made to date. District officials also credited state involvement and mandates with providing increased funding, technical support, and an "excuse" to improve leadership in their districts. We were not able to examine whether such systems improve student outcomes, and we acknowledge that cohesion can be built around ineffective policies and initiatives. But our analysis offers valuable insights on the importance of certain conditions for the ability of principals to engage in a range of practices to improve instruction in their schools.

In this chapter, we provide some practical lessons drawn from the experiences of the hundreds of people we interviewed who are engaged in this work. Although we focus on lessons learned about system-building for the purpose of improving school leadership, our recommendations are intended to be helpful to anyone engaged in developing closer working relationships between states and districts that can result in more-aligned policies for improving education.

Early Steps

Consider Local Contexts and Address the Challenges They Pose

States interested in developing CLSs would benefit from a close examination of their context and their capacity for the work. This study found that sites with a culture and history of collaboration and strong social networks were better suited for such efforts. Strong organizations and individuals who have the capacity and desire to lead system-building efforts and connect them to other reform efforts by virtue of their social capital are also important contextual conditions for success, as is a supportive political structure for public education reform. If states are taking the lead role in this work, selecting pilot districts in which the superintendent and the board members have aligned reform visions facilitates success. However, key challenges include limited resources, cultures of independence, and reform "burnout." Building cohesive systems under these conditions is more difficult. To ensure success in building cohesive systems and improving school leadership, sites may want to gauge how beneficial the local culture and political structure are and address any potential barriers before launching reform efforts.

Identify Strong Lead Organizations and Individuals

Although lead agencies in our study sites varied, the most advanced sites had in common a strategic approach to selecting the agency, and this distinguished them from most other sites. The advanced sites assessed the internal capacity of their SEAs, taking into account whether staff would be able to think and work outside the boundaries created by categorical federal programs, as well as the overall credibility of the SEAs and their political priorities. They then built distributed leadership systems in which several different types of organizations (e.g., universities, professional associations, regional offices, principal leadership academies, districts) held key lead roles. By contrast, several of the other states chose the SEA as the sole lead agency and came to believe that it did not have the staff or other resources to be effective.

Moreover, in advanced sites, strong leaders working from significant bases of power and influence had garnered political support for the importance of school leadership and the need to improve it. They also connected school leadership efforts to broader reform initiatives in the state, which helped sustain the leadership work and minimized burdens on schools and districts. Interviewees in the sites with the most advanced systems could easily point to these leaders, who have led the work for several years now. We recommend that state and district actors carefully consider the capacity of both individuals and organizations when selecting leaders to serve in coordinating roles.

Capitalize on External Expertise and Funding

Sites in our study engaged external organizations, notably The Wallace Foundation, but also others such as SREB, and key experts in school leadership to help them identify their capacity to create CLSs, as well as to assess where they stood on school leadership improvement efforts compared with similar sites. They used this information to identify areas of improvement and to benchmark their progress over time. The sites benefited greatly from The Wallace Foundation's funding as well. Securing similar levels of funding may be challenging, but local foundations near the study sites helped fund their work, both before and during the course of Wallace funding. We recommend that other sites investigate the array of monetary support and technical assistance available, including advice and guidance that the sites described in this report are willing to provide.

Implementation Phase

Build Trust and Mend Fences

We heard about many past and current acrimonious relationships between state and district actors. We also uncovered some approaches to building trust, such as acknowledging that the state and the districts are "in this together" and ensuring that state actors take the time to understand district contexts to develop the capacity to provide useful technical assistance. Although discord across organizations may be a significant barrier to building cohesion, it is possible to repair relationships between district and state actors, as Kentucky's experience proves. New state actors were able to repair relationships between district and state organizations in Georgia as well. Because there are undoubtedly many discordant relationships across the country, it may be important for new sites to establish trust among the state and district actors. Once trust has been established, it is easier to develop common understandings, shared goals, and joint ownership of the work.

Engage a Broad Coalition of Stakeholders

Across the study sites, building cohesion involved not only attending to policy and programmatic alignment within and across layers of the system, but also a process of engaging stakeholders and fostering agreement. Engagement required time and resources for coordination. It was also important to involve relevant stakeholders and give them the authority to make decisions, which fostered buy-in, rather than implementing new policies or initiatives without high levels of agreement. It was particularly important for the more cohesive sites to routinely gather key state and district leaders into the same room to collectively discuss leadership and develop policies and initiatives to improve it. Incentives were useful for garnering participation—several sites provided pilot funding to districts that were willing and able to take the lead in implementing leadership improvement programs. In addition, demonstrating that an initiative led to a desired outcome helped to convince others to join in the work. We recommend that sites wishing to develop CLSs explore strategies to ensure buy-in and foster agreement from as broad a portion of the educational community as possible. They may want to employ the strategies deemed successful by the study sites, or they may choose to develop their own.

Hone Skills at Applying Pressure While Providing Support

Although the study states reported struggling with the tension between providing support and holding districts accountable, those that were more successful in managing this tension also had more-advanced CLSs. To effectively apply pressure, state agencies had to be willing and able to exercise their powers. And state-provided support was effective only when state actors and agencies could provide the expertise that districts needed. Combining pressure with support is a strategy that should benefit both states and districts in any education endeavor, not just those focused on improving school leadership.

Recognize Innovative Districts as "Lead Learners"

Several states in our study recognized districts that were already doing important work on leadership development and used their innovations as models for other districts. They considered those districts "lead learners." States are well positioned to foster such innovations, evaluate their effectiveness, and spread them to other districts.

Connect Leadership Efforts to Standards and to Other Reforms in the State

Savvy leaders in the more-cohesive sites based their leadership reform efforts on statewide standards and connected their CLS-building efforts to other reforms in their states, such as high school and middle school reform programs. Leaders who were deeply socially networked were particularly successful in this realm. Sites would do well to employ this strategy, as it provides an anchor upon which to align policies and initiatives and might foster viability for leadership improvement work and sustainability in the future.

Evaluation, Sustainment, and Expansion

Solidify Programs and Funding Through Legislation and Regulations

Several of our study sites passed legislation and issued mandates to ensure implementation and funding of key leadership improvement efforts, such as mentoring, evaluation systems, and the redesign of pre-service programs. Although some interviewees worried about whether implementation would be faithful to the intent of the legislation, most celebrated the passing of legislation or mandates, describing these actions as critical steps in the overall reform effort.

Engage in Continuous Learning and Improvement

Respondents recommended that individuals and organizations involved in CLS-building seek and share expertise. In particular, they recommended participating in networks, attending conferences such as those supported by SREB and The Wallace Foundation, and referencing and conducting research. These types of activities helped sites determine how to move the work forward in their particular contexts. Some respondents reported the importance of collecting data to demonstrate that building a CLS had made a difference in their sites. These efforts were just starting in some sites but were likely to be important for attracting future funding.

Commit to Engaging in the Work over the Long Term

Many of the people we interviewed reported that building more-collaborative relationships between states and districts was hard work that required continuous effort. Four sites were able to implement only a few initiatives to improve leadership or build mature cohesive systems, despite receiving funding and support similar to that received by other sites. These states encountered many challenges, such as frequent turnover of key leaders, weak leaders and organizations in general, a history of discord across organizations, cultures of independence, or a lack of key political support. Even sites that had relatively advanced CLSs, like Iowa, reported that their accomplishments had taken years of hard work and were not easily achieved. A respondent from Iowa noted:

> I know in Iowa we are moving along, but even after the number of years we have had the Wallace funding, we are only now moving down the track at an acceptable speed. This kind of work takes a tremendous amount of time and only now do we have a clear direction and feel we are about to make a significant breakthrough at the state level.

Clearly, this work is not easy, and sites may not experience significant policy changes in their first few years of engaging stakeholders and coming to agreement on the importance of leadership and the most useful strategies for improving it in their state and districts. We hope that new sites recognize the level of effort that this work takes.

We also hope this monograph provides useful strategies and insights for state- and district-level officials who are willing to build the kind of broad collaboration that, given enough time and effort, can lead to significant policy changes.

Background Information on Study States and Districts

The states and districts examined in this study vary in a number of characteristics, including region of the United States, number of students enrolled in public schools, percentage of minorities, percentage of English-language learners, percentage of economically disadvantaged students, and whether the district is making AYP. The variation in sociodemographic characteristics and academic achievement provides an important contextual backdrop against which to compare the leadership improvement efforts of the sites and their progress toward building CLSs. This appendix provides a sociodemographic portrait of our study sites and displays trends in student achievement.

Sociodemographic Portrait

Table A.1 provides background information on the states and districts in the study. Each of the U.S. Census Bureau's four regions is represented: the Northeast (Massachusetts and Rhode Island), the South (Delaware, Georgia, and Kentucky), the Midwest (Illinois, Indiana, Iowa, and Missouri), and the West (Oregon). The states range in size of public school enrollment; together, they comprise 17 percent of the students educated in public schools in the United States.

Six of the 17 school districts (Atlanta, Boston, Chicago, Jefferson County, Portland, and St. Louis) are large urban districts, with enrollments in public schools ranging from about 38,000 students in St. Louis to more than 400,000 students in Chicago. Seven districts (Davenport, Eugene, Fort Wayne, Providence, Springfield (IL), Springfield (MA), and Waterloo) are located in smaller cities and have enrollments of between about 10,000 and 30,000 students. The remaining districts include Christina, which encompasses both a part of the city of Wilmington, DE, and the suburban town of Newark, NJ; Appoquinimink, which is centered in the small but fast-growing town of Middletown, DE; Indian River, a rural district in southern Delaware; and Clear Creek Amana, a very small, mostly rural district near Iowa City, IA.

Not surprisingly, the student demographics of the districts vary a great deal. Minority enrollment ranges from 9 percent in Clear Creek Amana to 92 percent in Chicago, while enrollment of economically disadvantaged students ranges from 14 per-

Table A.1
Demographic Portrait of Study Sites in 2007

Site	Number of Districts in State	Number of Schools in State	Urban Designation of District	Student Enrollment (total/% of state)	% Minority	% English-Language Learners	% Eligible for Free/Reduced Lunch—Economically Disadvantaged
Delaware	19	234		122,254	46.0	5.5	37.0
Appoquinimink			Town, fringe	7,588 (6.2)	29.9	2.1	13.5
Christina			Suburb, large	18,495 (15.1)	59.2	7.3	38.6
Indian River			Town, distant	8,138 (6.6)	36.7	7.4	44.6
Georgia	182	2,463		1,629,157	53.1	4.0	50.3
Atlanta			City, large	50,631 (3.1)	91.1	2.2	74.9
Illinois	875	4,392		2,118,276	45.3	9.3	38.8
Chicago			City, large	413,694 (19.5)	91.9	16.4	75.3
Springfield			City, midsize	14,875 (0.7)	45.7	0.4	58.4
Indiana	295	1,969		1,045,940	23.2	4.2	37.3
Fort Wayne			City, midsize	31,884 (3.0)	43.8	5.3	56.5
Iowa	365	1,509		483,122[b]	14.9[b]	3.8	33.4[b]
Clear Creek Amana			Rural, distant	1,438[b] (0.3)	8.8[b]	0.2[a]	20.2[b]
Davenport			City, small	16,275 (3.4)	34.9	1.9[a]	50.5[b]
Waterloo			City, small	10,590 (2.2)	38.4	5.5[a]	49.4[b]
Kentucky	176	1,534		683,173	20.2	1.6	48.5
Jefferson County			City, large	91,425 (13.4)	45.5	4.3[a]	25.9[c]
Massachusetts	356	1,879		968,661	28.5	5.8	28.5
Boston			City, large	56,388 (5.8)	86.5	18.3	72.7

Table A.1 (continued)

Site	Number of Districts in State	Number of Schools in State	Urban Designation of District	Student Enrollment (total/% of state)	% Minority	% English-Language Learners	% Eligible for Free/Reduced Lunch—Economically Disadvantaged
Springfield			City, midsize	27,791 (2.9)	81.7	13.7	77.5
Missouri	524	2,384		920,353	23.7	2.0	41.8
St. Louis			City, large	38,277 (4.2)	86.7	14.0	73.8
Oregon	199	1,284		562,574	29.6	11.2	41.3
Eugene			City, midsize	17,896 (3.2)	27.3	2.6	30.8
Portland			City, large	44,478 (7.9)	44.6	12.0	45.3
Rhode Island	32	336		151,612	30.5	6.6	32.7
Providence			City, midsize	24,922 (16.4)	88.0	21.2	66.5
Nation	14,556	100,308		49,843,083	45.0	5.0	41.8

SOURCE: CCSSO, 2009.

NOTE: City, large = a territory inside an urbanized area and inside a principal city with a population of 250,000 or more. City, midsize = a territory inside an urbanized area and inside a principal city with a population of less than 250,000 and more than or equal to 100,000. City, small = a territory inside an urbanized area and inside a principal city with a population of less than 100,000. Suburb, large = a territory outside a principal city and inside an urbanized area with a population of 250,000 or more. Town, fringe = a territory inside an urban cluster that is less than or equal to 10 miles from an urbanized area. Town, distant = a territory inside an urban cluster that's more than 10 miles and less than or equal to 35 miles from an urbanized area. Rural, distant = U.S. Census–defined rural territory that is more than 5 miles but less than or equal to 25 miles from an urbanized area, as well as rural territory that is more than 2.5 miles but less than or equal to 10 miles from an urban cluster.

[a]Common Core of Data (CCD), 2006–2007, National Center for Education Statistics (NCES), U.S. Department of Education, 2009.

[b]Figures are for 2008.

[c]Figure is for 2006.

cent in Appoquinimink to 78 percent in Springfield (MA). Most of the districts could be characterized as greatly challenged. Twelve of the 17 districts have a greater percentage of economically disadvantaged students than the nation as a whole, and nine have a greater percentage of English-language learners. Six of the districts (Atlanta, Boston, Chicago, Providence, Springfield (MA), and St. Louis) have especially high-needs student populations. Each of these six districts has over 80 percent minority enrollment, and two-thirds or more of the students are economically disadvantaged.

Trends in Adequate Yearly Progress

Table A.2 shows whether each district in our study met AYP on the state's student assessments from 2004 to 2008.[1] This information is important for understanding how districts are performing relative to the state's educational standards and what kind of performance pressures the district may be under. According to NCLB legislation, districts that fail to meet a state's AYP targets are considered to be "in need of improvement." If the district fails to achieve AYP two years after it was first identified as being in need of improvement, the state may take a number of actions, including deferring program funds or reducing administrative funds, removing the district's staff, removing schools from the district's jurisdiction, or permitting students to transfer to other districts. Only two of our study districts (Clear Creek Amana and Indian River) met AYP consistently during the five years we tracked.

Trends in National Assessment of Educational Progress Scores

We compared achievement across states with data from the National Assessment of Educational Progress (NAEP). According to the NAEP website, "The National Assessment of Educational Progress . . . is the only nationally representative and continuing assessment of what America's students know and can do in various subject areas."[2] NAEP, often called "the Nation's Report Card," is periodically administered to a sample of students in each state, enabling comparisons across time and across states. For this analysis, we collected average scale scores in fourth- and eighth-grade math and reading for the 10 states in the study, as well as NAEP's nationally representative

---

[1] NCLB required all states to test students in grades 3 through 8 plus a high school grade to develop timelines to bring all students to proficiency by 2014 and to establish a system to determine which schools and districts are failing to make AYP. States were given several years of transition to expand their testing systems to cover all required grades and to determine benchmarks against which AYP would be measured. A state's determination of a district's AYP is based on whether the district is meeting designated performance targets. This definition differs across states.

[2]   National Center for Education Statistics, nd.

Table A.2
Study Districts' AYP Status (2004–2008)

State/District	Made AYP in 2004	Made AYP in 2005	Made AYP in 2006	Made AYP in 2007	Made AYP in 2008
Delaware					
Appoquinimink	Yes	Yes	Yes	No	No
Christina	Yes	No	Yes	No	No
Indian River	Yes	Yes	Yes	Yes	Yes
Georgia					
Atlanta	No	No	No	No	No
Illinois					
Chicago	No	No	No	No	No
Springfield	No	No	No	No	No
Indiana					
Fort Wayne	No	No	No	No	NA
Iowa					
Clear Creek Amana	Yes	Yes	Yes	Yes	Yes
Davenport	No	No	No	Yes	No
Waterloo	No	No	No	Yes	No
Kentucky					
Jefferson County	No	No	No	No	No
Massachusetts					
Boston	No	No	No	No	No
Springfield	No	No	No	No	No
Missouri					
St. Louis	No	No	No	No	No
Oregon					
Eugene	No	No	No	No	No
Portland	No	No	No	No	No
Rhode Island[a]					
Providence	No	(a)	No	No	No

SOURCE: State department of education websites.
NOTE: NA = not available.
[a] In 2005, Rhode Island administered high school exams only; it made no district designation of AYP.

public school sample in 2003 and 2007. The most recent NAEP results were from 2007. We chose 2003 as a comparison year because it was the first year in which all the states in our study participated in both the reading and math assessments. Data were downloaded using the NAEP Data Explorer tool on the NAEP website.

Tables A.3 and A.4 display the average scale scores in fourth- and eighth-grade math and reading in 2007 and the difference from 2003 to 2007 between each state's

Table A.3
2007 NAEP Scale Scores for 4th and 8th Grade Math and Reading

State	Grade 4 Math		Grade 4 Reading		Grade 8 Math		Grade 8 Reading	
	Avg. Scale Score	Difference Between State and National Scale Scores	Avg. Scale Score	Difference Between State and National Scale Scores	Avg. Scale Score	Difference Between State and National Scale Scores	Avg. Scale Score	Difference Between State and National Scale Scores
Delaware	242	3*	225	5*	283	3*	265	4*
Georgia	235	−4*	219	−1	275	−5*	259	−2*
Illinois	237	−2	219	−1	280	0	263	2
Indiana	245	6*	222	2	285	5*	264	3*
Iowa	243	4*	225	5*	285	5*	267	6*
Kentucky	235	−4*	222	2*	279	−1	262	1
Massachusetts	252	13*	236	16*	298	18*	273	12*
Missouri	239	0	221	1	281	1	263	2*
Oregon	236	−3*	215	−5*	284	4*	266	5*
Rhode Island	236	−3*	219	−1	275	−5*	258	−3*
Nation	239	NA	220	NA	280	NA	261	NA

NOTE: An asterisk signifies that the difference between the state scale score and the national scale score is statistically significant.

Table A.4
Change in Average Scale Scores from 2003 to 2007

State	Grade 4 Math			Grade 8 Math			Grade 4 Reading			Grade 8 Reading		
	2003 Avg. Scale Score	2007 Avg. Scale Score	Chg.	2003 Avg. Scale Score	2007 Avg. Scale Score	Chg.	2003 Avg. Scale Score	2007 Avg. Scale Score	Chg.	2003 Avg. Scale Score	2007 Avg. Scale Score	Chg.
Delaware	236	242	6*	277	283	6*	224	225	1	265	265	0
Georgia	230	235	5*	270	275	5*	214	219	5*	258	259	1
Illinois	233	237	4*	277	280	3*	216	219	3	266	263	−4*
Indiana	238	245	7*	281	285	4*	220	222	1	265	264	−1
Iowa	238	243	4*	284	285	1	223	225	2	268	267	0
Kentucky	229	235	6*	274	279	4*	219	222	3	266	262	−4*
Massachusetts	242	252	11*	287	298	11*	228	236	8*	273	273	0
Missouri	235	239	5*	279	281	2	222	221	−1	267	263	−4*
Oregon	236	236	0	281	284	3	218	215	−3	264	266	2
Rhode Island	230	236	6*	272	275	3*	216	219	2	261	258	−3*
Nation	234	239	5*	276	280	4*	216	220	4*	261	261	0

NOTE: An asterisk signifies that the change in scale score from 2003 to 2007 is statistically significant.

average scale score and the national average scale score for each grade and subject. Differences marked with an asterisk in the tables are statistically significant, as tested by NAEP.[3]

As Table A.3 shows, there was a great deal of variation in results on the NAEP test across the states in our study in 2007. Georgia and Rhode Island achieved at lower levels than the national sample, while Delaware, Indiana, and Iowa performed at higher levels than the national sample. Massachusetts was by far the highest performer in 2007, with achievement levels considerably higher than the national sample. Kentucky was a high achiever in fourth-grade reading but a low achiever in fourth-grade math. Oregon performed well on the middle school assessments but below the national sample on the elementary-level assessments.

Table A.4 shows that, in general, math achievement increased from 2003 to 2007 in the states, as well as the nation as a whole, and most of these changes were statistically significant. Again, Massachusetts took the lead, increasing its average scale score in fourth- and eighth-grade math by 11 points in each case. The story in reading achievement was very different. Although fourth-grade reading improved in the nation as a whole from 2003 to 2007, it improved in only two of the 10 states in the study, Georgia and Massachusetts. Achievement in eighth-grade reading remained the same in the nation and either remained the same or decreased in the study states.

---

[3] We report the results of statistical tests produced by the NAEP Data Explorer. NAEP uses t-tests, and differences are reported as significant if they meet the 5 percent threshold.

Indicators of Leadership Policy Initiatives, Factors of Cohesion, Conditions, and Effective Leadership Practices

The Wallace Foundation's hypothesis asserts that one element of a CLS is a set of conditions and incentives that support effective leadership, including necessary data to inform decisions, authority to direct needed resources (people, time, and money), and policies governing recruitment, hiring, placement, and evaluation of school leaders that support student learning goals. The Foundation suggests that states and districts should act to put these conditions in place. During our first site visit (to Chicago and Springfield, IL) we asked site representatives about their efforts in this regard. Their responses suggested that there might be conditions that influence the effectiveness of leaders in addition to those outlined in the CLS hypothesis. Therefore, we conducted a review of the literature on school leadership and school improvement to generate a more detailed list of conditions that research suggests might support effective leadership. This list, provided below, was used to guide revisions of interview protocols and the development of our study's online survey and logs.

I. Policies and Initiatives on Standards, Training, and Conditions

1. Number, types, and reach of policies, programs, legislation, etc.
   a. Standards
   b. Evaluation
   c. Training
      i. Pre-service preparation
         1. Improving recruitment
         2. Improving content of programs
         3. Providing internships
         4. Providing mentoring
      ii. In-service PD
         1. In-service/induction
         2. Mentoring
         3. PD

    d. Licensure
       i. Provisional license
      ii. Initial leader licensure/certification
     iii. Relicensure/certification/professional licensure
     iv. Advanced license/master principal
    e. Conditions (see list under III below)
       i. Principal autonomy
      ii. Data use and monitoring
     iii. Resource allocation
     iv. Curriculum and instruction
      v. Interventions for low-performing schools and students
     vi. Staff selection, PD, and effectiveness
    vii. Governance
   viii. Parent and community engagement
    ix. School culture

Strategies for implementing leadership actions
    a. Technical assistance
    b. Communications strategy
    c. Informal coalitions/formal commissions or task forces
    d. Technological tools

Enabling and impeding factors for actions
    a. Capacity of state-level entities
    b. Leadership
    c. Turnover
    d. Resources (time and money)
    e. Involvement of stakeholder
    f. Political culture

Sustainability and other remaining challenges for actions
    a. Changes to legislation or other formal policy
    b. Sustainable funding (e.g., budget line item)
    c. Institutionalization of leadership staff or departments

II. Cohesion in Standards, Training, and Conditions Across a Site (Study Districts Within a State)

  1. Structural components of cohesion
    a. Comprehensiveness of leadership improvement policies and initiatives
       i. That follow the career continuum of school leaders (from pre-service through retirement)

      ii. That encompass the gamut of school leaders (from teacher leaders through school boards)

   b. Extent of alignment

      i. Among leadership improvement actions

      ii. Between leadership improvement actions and broader actions to improve student achievement

2. Process components of cohesion

   a. Breadth of engagement of stakeholders

   b. Extent to which actions represent a common vision of leadership (what leaders should know and be able to do)

   c. Extent of coordination

      i. Presence of a clear coordinating body

      ii. Evidence of a coordinated effort over a sustained period of time

      iii. Strategic use of resources, coordinated with actions

Strategies for building cohesion

   a. Dedicated time for joint goal-setting/planning/taking action

   b. Inclusion of multiple stakeholders

   c. Clear communication among stakeholders

   d. Use of experts/consultants to shape vision

Enabling and impeding factors for cohesion

   a. Skilled/legitimate/stable leadership

   b. Political culture

   c. Policy context

   d. Salience of leadership

Sustainability and other remaining challenges for cohesion

   a. Legislation

   b. Common language across state/districts

   c. Staff dedicated to maintaining cohesion

III. Elaborated List of Conditions That Support Principal Effectiveness

1. Principals have *autonomy* for

   a. Determining the school calendar and daily schedule

   b. Selecting curricula, textbooks, and other instructional materials

   c. Determining content of PD programs for teachers

   d. Evaluating teachers

   e. Hiring new full-time teachers

   f. Hiring new full-time school administrators (e.g., assistant principals)

   g. Removing and disciplining teachers

    h. Matching teachers' skills with student learning needs
    i. Setting and enforcing student discipline policy
    j. Deciding how monetary resources will be spent
    k. Freedom from overly burdensome district/state mandates and regulations
    l. Freedom to select technical assistance and PD targeted to the leader's needs

2. Principals have support for *data use and monitoring*, including
    a. Assessments aligned with state and district standards
    b. Common or benchmark assessments administered on a frequent basis to monitor student progress toward standards
    c. Timely feedback on student performance
    d. Accurate, valid, and reliable data for making decisions about individual students
    e. Multiple performance measures to assess student learning
    f. Training on how to access and analyze data for school improvement
    g. Strategies and opportunities to engage teachers, parents, and other stakeholders in assessing progress

3. District, state, and/or other fiscal administrator manages *resources* such that
    a. Resources are targeted toward closing the achievement gap (i.e., more resources for low-performing schools)
    b. Resources are allocated to proven/effective or research-based programs
    c. Resource allocations are based on school and student needs
    d. Additional resources/incentives for hard-to-staff schools, hard-to-staff subject areas (may require state or union approval)
    e. Incentives (such as differential teacher compensation) provided for improved student outcomes
    f. Incentives (such as licensure reciprocity and/or pension portability) provided to assure supply to meet demand for high-quality teachers and leaders

4. District (or other administrative entity) *curriculum and instruction policies* that provide
    a. Instructional programs that help students meet standards
    b. Research-based curricula aligned with state and district standards
    c. Sufficient resources (materials, time, and staff) to implement programs
    d. Sufficient PD and technical assistance to implement programs
    e. Interventions, strategies, and training for differentiated instruction
    f. Principals' ability to access technical assistance from district staff and/or intermediary organizations regarding curriculum issues

5. District (or other administrative entity) *policies for low-performing schools and students* that provide
   a. Availability of effective, research-based interventions
   b. Additional resources for high-need schools
   c. Outside support and assistance from district or state support teams/mentors/coaches or intermediary organizations to build staff capacity and implement plans

6. District (or other administrative entity) *personnel policies* that provide
   a. An effective and efficient recruitment and hiring process to attract high-quality teachers and leaders
   b. Targeted, timely, high-quality PD that meets the needs of individuals and schools
   c. Adequate time for teacher PD
   d. Support for new teachers (coaches, mentors, master teachers)
   e. Opportunity and time to form professional learning communities
   f. A succession plan for school leaders
   g. A fair, evidence-based process for teacher or leader dismissal
   h. Principals' ability to access technical assistance from district staff and/or intermediary organizations regarding staff selection, PD, and evaluation issues

7. Governance *policies and structures* that
   a. Support the district vision and goals
   b. Clearly define roles and responsibilities of governing entities and prevent district and school governing boards from interfering with district and school leader autonomy
   c. Encourage the school board and teachers' union to focus on school improvement
   d. Coordinate governing entities to assure role alignment and mutual accountability
   e. Encourage stakeholder and parent engagement in district and school policy, practice, and improvement decisions
   f. Encourage distributed leadership throughout the district

8. *School context and culture* [principals should be able to influence school culture in the long term, but we anticipate that school context and culture will influence whether and how principals enact effective leadership practices in the short term]
   a. Collaborative work across a school
   b. Joint responsibility for student success

      c. A well-developed process for ongoing schoolwide improvement and planning

      d. Teachers open to change

      e. Distributed leadership throughout the school

      f. Strong parent and community engagement

      g. Probably other conditions

IV. Principals Exhibiting Behaviors and Values of Effective School Leaders

  1. Development and implementation of strategic goals and school improvement efforts

      a. Building a common vision

      b. School improvement efforts

  2. Supporting the instruction of students

      a. Ensuring a supportive learning environment

      b. Motivating students

      c. Monitoring classroom instruction

      d. Engaging with teachers outside of the classroom

  3. Promoting the development and leadership of the school's teachers and staff

      a. Promoting staff PD

      b. Motivating staff

      c. Developing leadership teams

V. State Role

  1. Shaping state universities/educational leadership programming

  2. Setting policies that affect how prospective principals are recruited, selected, trained, and licensed

  3. Shaping the local conditions within which principals lead schools

  4. Allocating resources (funding, staff, new infrastructure) toward leadership development

  5. Bringing attention to the issue of school leadership

  6. Providing processes and structures that enable alignment/coherence

  7. Monitoring and evaluating efforts to improve school leadership

Principal Survey Technical Notes

Survey Administration

As part of the effort to collect principals' perspectives on their conditions, time they spent on leadership practices, and whether they felt the time spent was appropriate, we administered an online survey from May through June 2008. Contact information for each school and principal was obtained from school district websites. We created principal lists that included the principal's name, principal's e-mail address, school name, school address, and phone number; we then sent the lists to the relevant school districts to verify their accuracy. The lists were used to administer the principal survey and conduct follow-up activities.

We staggered the launch of the survey to correspond with the end of the school year for each district—after state testing was completed, but prior to the last days of school. In some cases, we changed launch dates to accommodate requests made by district staff. One week prior to the launch of the survey, principals in all districts except one received an e-mail from a district representative encouraging them to complete the survey. Following the district e-mail, a RAND team member sent each principal an e-mail that described the survey and included a link to the survey website.

We administered four follow-up efforts to ensure that the principals filled out the survey. Those who failed to respond to the survey after the first e-mail received a reminder e-mail one week after the launch. Those who failed to respond two weeks after the launch received a second reminder e-mail and were mailed a hardcopy version, which they were asked to mail back to RAND, or they could follow the directions in an enclosed letter to connect to the survey's website. We then called all remaining nonresponders. Some districts where response rates were particularly low also received additional reminder e-mails.

In addition to this multistage process, we asked districts if they would allow us to administer the survey during professional retreats or principal meetings. Atlanta, Providence, and St. Louis agreed to do so, and this strategy was very helpful in raising our response rates. Nonresponders were not singled out at these events, and principals were reminded that the survey was voluntary. Many of our district contacts also agreed to send further e-mails or memos to their principals to encourage them to complete the survey.

Before analyzing the survey data, we removed anomalies (such as duplicate responses, incorrectly assigned IDs, or errors in the data transfer from the online survey to the dataset downloaded from the website). We also dropped 20 respondents from the database who were assistant principals or other administrators who had completed the survey instead of the principal. A total of 598 responses remained after data cleaning was complete. Table C.1 displays the final response rates.

Weights

Because of the relatively low overall response rate (39 percent) and the variation in response rates across districts, we assessed whether the final sample was representative of the population of principals in our districts, on the basis of the mean percentage of socioeconomically disadvantaged students; total enrollment; percentage of Hispanic students; percentage of African-American students; school-level math and reading proficiency rates; and the number of respondents who led a high school, middle school, or elementary school for the total school population over all districts and for the schools

Table C.1
Principal Survey Response Rates by District

School District	Number of Survey Respondents	Total Number of Principals	Response Rate (%)
Appoquinimink, DE	8	11	73
Atlanta, GA	92	100	92
Boston, MA	33	150	22
Chicago, IL	105	617	17
Christina, DE	24	29	83
Clear Creek, IA	4	4	100
Davenport, IA	21	28	75
Eugene, OR	27	36	75
Fort Wayne, IN	33	55	60
Indian River, DE	12	13	92
Jefferson County, KY	58	151	38
Portland, OR	62	98	63
Providence, RI	30	47	64
Springfield, IL	20	33	61
Springfield, MA	14	44	32
St. Louis, MO	44	88	50
Waterloo, IA	11	20	55
Total	598	1,524	39

of our sample of principals. We found differences between the population and the sample in a number of important categories (Table C.2). Our responding principals tended to be from schools with higher socioeconomic status (65 percent economically disadvantaged in the sample versus 71 percent in the population), lower enrollment (584 versus 635 mean total enrollment), and higher achievement (63 percent versus 57 percent proficient or better in reading and 61 percent versus 57 percent proficient or better in math). In addition, enrollment of Hispanic and African-American students was lower in the schools of our responding principals than in the population.

We then ran a logistic regression in which the dependent variable was response (1 for response, 0 for nonresponse) and the independent variables were the school socioeconomic, demographic, and achievement characteristics described above and indicators for school level. We also accounted for school district variation in response and included indicators for the districts. We used the results of the logistic regression to generate predicted values of response and created weights for each case based on the inverse of these predicted values. The goal of this weighting was to up-weight principals in the sample who resemble the nonresponding principals so that the sample more closely resembles the population. Principals who were overrepresented, based on the characteristics above, were concomitantly down-weighted relative to the underrepresented principals.

We generated three sets of nonresponse weights, which we used in the analyses. One set of weights was for the entire sample of principals, one set was for principals in the CLS states, and one set was for principals in the non-CLS states. In our analyses of all the principal responses, we used the entire-sample nonresponse weights, because our population of interest was principals across all the states. For the separate analyses of the CLS and non-CLS states, because our populations of interest were restricted to those states, we used the nonresponse weights generated for only them.

Table C.2
Differences in School Characteristics Between the Population and Sample of Responding Principals

Variable	Population Mean (total schools in all districts)	Sample Mean (schools of responding principals)
Total enrollment	635	584
Enrollment of economically disadvantaged (%)	71	65
Hispanic enrollment (%)	23	18
African-American enrollment (%)	47	43
Students proficient in reading (%)	57	63
Students proficient in mathematics (%)	57	61

NOTE: Percentages are rounded; differences are significant at the 0.05 level.

The use of a small selection of variables in constructing the weights may have affected the weights' precision. However, it enabled us to minimize the number of cases we would lose because of missing information. It is important to note that other variables might account for nonresponse bias in our data; principal practices are not necessarily directly linked to a school's demographic and achievement characteristics. To test the accuracy of our weights, we compared the means of the school characteristics for the weighted sample and the population of principals in our study districts. We included comparisons on the following school characteristics which we did not use as part of the weighting scheme:

- Title I–eligible school
- Schoolwide Title I eligibility
- 2007 reading proficiency for African-American students
- 2007 reading proficiency for Hispanic students
- 2007 reading proficiency for economically disadvantaged students
- 2007 math proficiency for African-American students
- 2007 math proficiency for Hispanic students
- 2007 math proficiency for economically disadvantaged students.

We found that after nonresponse weighting, the means of the school characteristics of the principals for the entire sample closely resembled those of the population of principals across all states.[1] The one variable that does not perform as well is Hispanic proficiency in both math and reading. Those variables may have more missing observations than the others, and it is therefore difficult to balance the sample to the population on them.

In general, using weights in our analyses causes standard errors to increase. This is likely to result in underestimating the significance of the results. However, the estimates yield less-biased results than they would have if we had chosen not to construct and use the weights.

---

[1] We found this to be the case for the means of the population of principals in only the CLS states. We did not find this to be the case for the nonresponse weights generated for only the non-CLS principals. This is likely because the population of non-CLS principals is smaller than that of CLS principals. The precision of the covariates to create nonresponse weights for that sample only is likely to be less than that of the entire principal sample or just the CLS states.

Principal End-of-Day-Log Technical Notes

Log Development

The goal of the end-of-day logs was to gather daily perspectives of principals on the amount of time they were able to spend on leadership practices focused on developing and advancing students' learning.

The end-of-day logs were divided into three sections. The first asked principals to indicate the time they spent on a number of activities typically performed during a working day. These included building operations, financial support for the school, community or parent relations, school district functions, student affairs, personnel issues, planning and setting goals, professional growth, and instructional leadership. The second section asked principals about particular conditions that enabled or hindered their engagement in five instructional leadership practices: school improvement planning or developing goals; planning and/or leading teachers' PD; supervising, counseling, and evaluating staff; monitoring, observing, and/or providing feedback on instruction; and analyzing student data or student work. The third section asked principals to provide an example from that day in which a condition either greatly hindered or greatly increased their ability to advance student learning.

For the purposes of this study, we analyzed the response to the third section and created an Excel spreadsheet in which responses were categorized into various groups of practices and then by enabling and inhibiting conditions.

Sample Selection and Administration

Principals we targeted for the end-of-day logs were those whom the district designated as relatively high-performing. Our rationale was similar to the one used for our principal interviews: If high-performing principals noted that particular conditions were impeding or enabling their work, other principals were likely to be facing similar obstacles or support structures. Like the sample of interviewed principals, the principals chosen to fill out the end-of-day logs may pose selection-bias issues. These data do not allow us to examine conditions or leadership practices of struggling principals, which may differ in type or scope from those encountered by higher-performing principals.

End-of-day log surveys were administered daily to each of the targeted principals for one week in October 2008 and one week in November 2008. One hundred sixty-seven principals completed at least one, and as many as 10, logs during this period. Table D.1 shows the final response rates after the data were cleaned.

Table D.1
Response Rates for End-of-Day Logs

School District	Number of Responses	Total Number Targeted Across 10 Days	Response Rate (%)
Appoquinimink, DE	48	120	40.00
Atlanta, GA	134	150	89.33
Boston, MA	157	260	60.38
Chicago, IL	61	250	24.40
Christina, DE	76	240	31.67
Clear Creek, IA	33	40	82.50
Davenport, IA	89	190	46.84
Eugene, OR	83	150	55.33
Ft. Wayne, IN	113	150	75.33
Indian River, DE	55	140	39.29
Jefferson County, KY	105	180	58.33
Portland, OR	80	150	53.33
Providence, RI	83	150	55.33
Springfield, IL	88	160	55.00
Springfield, MA	103	160	64.38
St. Louis, MO	57	200	28.50
Waterloo, IA	31	200	15.50
Total	1,396	2,890	48.30

Index Construction for the Analyses in Chapter Eight

The analyses in Chapter Eight assess the relationship between principals' reported conditions and time spent on instructional leadership practices and whether principals feel that the time is appropriate and sufficient. To conduct the analyses, we created indices for four of the eight analyzed conditions and all nine of the instructional leadership practices. The time-spent and perceptions-of-time-spent indices parallel each other: Each index of time spent is accompanied by an index constructed of items asking the principal's opinion on whether the time spent on a particular activity is appropriate and sufficient.

These indices capture broad categories of conditions and instructional leadership practices that the literature indicates are important determinants of effective school leadership. In this appendix, we describe how we constructed the indices.

Using information obtained in a review of the literature, we grouped survey items asking principals about the conditions they encountered in their daily working lives and the instructional leadership activities they practiced into broad categories. We then tested our theoretical grouping through confirmatory factor analysis and found that the groupings held together well.

Tables E.1 and E.2 present the broad categories of conditions, time spent, and perceptions about the appropriateness of time spent; the associated survey items; and the Cronbach alpha, a measure of the reliability of a newly formed variable. A Cronbach alpha of 0.8 is generally considered to be an indication that the newly constructed variable is robust. The alphas for the conditions indices range from 0.75 to 0.85. The time-spent indices range from 0.57 to 0.83. Those for perceptions of appropriateness of time spent range from 0.62 to 0.80. Although the alphas for the indices of instructional leadership practices are less robust than those for the conditions, we are confident of the theoretical underpinnings for combining these items. As a further check on the reliability of the index construction, we conducted regression analyses using both the instructional-leadership-practice indices and individual items as the dependent variables. In general, we found the findings with individual items (not shown) to be consistent with those of our analyses using the indices.

Table E.1
Indices for Conditions, Associated Items, Scale, and Alphas

Index Variable	Associated Items	Scale	Alpha
Data (state and district)	• Timely • Organized • Accurate and easily accessible • Accurate and reliable • Results are useful	0 (strongly disagree) to 3 (strongly agree)	0.85
Resources	• Resources to meet student academic needs • Resources to meet student social and emotional needs • Adequacy of facilities and transportation • Sufficient time and staff support	0 (strongly disagree) to 3 (strongly agree)	0.75
Quality of district-provided evaluation and PD	• Tools and training on data • Professional development for principals • Evaluations based on state leadership standards • Evaluations focused on instructional leadership • Evaluations use clear and transparent criteria • Access to technical assistance	0 (not at all) to 3 (to a large extent)	0.87
Autonomy (authority)	• Set achievement goals • Set daily schedule • Establish curriculum • Select textbooks • Budget • Hire teachers • Evaluate teachers • Remove teachers • Hire administrators • Remove administrators	0 (no authority) to 3 (complete authority)	0.81

NOTE: Four of the conditions used in the analyses for Chapter Eight are items not listed in this table.

Table E.2
Indices for Instructional Leadership Practices, Associated Items, and Alphas

Index Variable	Associated Items	Alpha
Building a common vision	• Developing, implementing, and monitoring strategic goals • Assisting staff in developing a shared vision • Involving parents in supporting school strategic goals	Time spent: 0.78 Appropriateness of time spent: 0.76
School improvement	• Monitoring the phase-in of school improvement efforts • Using data to monitor school progress • Aligning human and fiscal resources to strategic priorities	Time spent: 0.59 Appropriateness of time spent: 0.64
Creating a supportive learning environment for students	• Establishing a safe and orderly environment • Minimize disruptions of instructional time	Time spent: 0.57 Appropriateness of time spent: 0.62
Motivating students	• Communicating high expectations to students • Providing incentives for students • Acknowledging students	Time spent: 0.67 Appropriateness of time spent: 0.72
Monitoring classroom instruction	• Organizing classroom walkthroughs • Collecting and examining student work • Reviewing and providing feedback on teacher lesson plans	Time spent: 0.67 Appropriateness of time spent: 0.72
Engaging with teachers outside of the classroom to improve the instruction of students	• Creating opportunities for staff collaboration • Holding teachers accountable for student academic progress • Setting up systems for teachers to examine student work in relation to grade-level expectations and/or state standards • Informing teachers of the school's performance on state and district assessments • Guiding the development and evaluation of curriculum that is aligned with local and state standards and assessments	Time spent: 0.73 Appropriateness of time spent: 0.74
Promoting staff PD	• Working with individual staff members to evaluate professional needs and capacities • Arranging high-quality PD for staff • Helping staff members find resources to accomplish their professional goals • Working with staff to use achievement data for decisionmaking	Time spent: 0.66 Appropriateness of time spent: 0.71
Stimulating and motivating staff	• Stimulating staff to consider how they could carry out their work more effectively • Communicating high expectations for staff • Acknowledging exceptional staff effort and/or performance	Time spent: 0.64 Appropriateness of time spent: 0.68
Fostering leadership among staff	• Establishing and developing school leadership teams • Developing leadership capacity of staff • Encouraging individual, small-team, and whole-school problem-solving	Time spent: 0.83 Appropriateness of time spent: 0.80

NOTE: For all indices, the time-spent index was coded from 0 (no time or some time) to 1 (a great deal of time); the feelings-about-time-spent index was coded from 0 (not sufficient or excessive) to 1 (appropriate and sufficient).

Methodology and Elaborated Results for Analyses in Chapter Eight

In this appendix we describe the data sources used for the analyses presented in Chapter Eight. We detail the methodology used to test the mean differences between principals in CLS and non-CLS sites and the ordinary least squares (OLS) regression analyses. This appendix also presents the results from the mean-difference tests and the regression analyses.

Data Sources

We compiled school-level socioeconomic, demographic, and achievement information from multiple sources. We used these variables to estimate response weights and as controls for school-level factors in our examination of support for the CLS hypothesis. From the NCES Common Core of Data (CCD) website we downloaded school geographic information (such as address and contact information), school level and grade span, measures of economic disadvantage, school type (such as traditional public, charter, or public magnet), and total enrollment, as well as the NCES unique school identifier.

We downloaded additional socioeconomic, demographic, and achievement variables on each school from SchoolDataDirect (SDD), an online source of education data that is sponsored by the non-profit CCSSO and administered by Standard and Poor's. SDD maintains a host of education data from federal, state, and district sources.

Table F.1 summarizes the variables we utilized in our analyses, with a brief description of each, the academic year to which it pertains, and its source. We used these data as control variables in our logistic regression to generate the sample nonresponse weights. We also used them as controls in our OLS regressions examining the impact of principals' reported conditions on time spent and their feelings about time spent. We used the most recent year for which data were both available and complete.

Table F.1
Analysis Data Sources

Variable	Description	Academic Year	Primary Source	Original Source for SDD Data
School level	Primary, middle, high, or other	2005–2006	NCES CCD	NA
Total student enrollment	Total number of students enrolled in school	2005–2006	NCES CCD	NA
Enrollment of economically disadvantaged students	Percentage of students classified as economically disadvantaged	2006–2007	SDD	NCES and state departments of education
Math proficiency	SDD-calculated percentage of students meeting or exceeding state proficiency standards in math, using state-reported data on number of students meeting proficient or above and number of students who took the test	2007–2008 or 2006–2007 where 2007–2008 was not available	SDD	State departments of education
Reading proficiency	SDD-calculated percentage of students meeting or exceeding state proficiency standards in reading, using state-reported data on number of students meeting proficient or above and number of students who took the test	2007–2008 or 2006–2007 where 2007–2008 was not available	SDD	State departments of education
Hispanic enrollment	Percentage of Hispanic students in the school	2006–2007	SDD	NCES and state departments of education
African-American enrollment	Percentage of African-American students in the school	2006–2007	SDD	NCES and state departments of education

Means Tests

In this section, we describe in detail the methodology we used to examine differences between reports from principals in CLS and non-CLS sites and present the means for the indices described in Appendix E and for each survey item used to construct the indices.

Calculating Means and Standard Errors of Outcome Indices and Survey Items for CLS and Non-CLS Principals

The means and standard errors of CLS and non-CLS principal reports on the survey items and the composite indices were calculated while factoring in the complex survey design and our need to adjust for survey nonresponse. To examine the means and standard errors of responses for principals in CLS sites and non-CLS sites, we used the nonresponse weights calculated using only the population of CLS principals and only the population of non-CLS sites. Because we were examining what principals in CLS and non-CLS sites reported separately, it is appropriate to consider them as separate populations. In this case, we considered the primary sampling unit to be the principal and the strata to be the school district. The same principle applied when we examined the means and standard errors of the non-CLS principal population. We used non-response weights specifically developed for CLS principals and non-CLS principals (see Appendix D).

Examining Whether Principal-Reported Outcomes Differ Between CLS and Non-CLS States

In addition to examining the means and standard errors of CLS and non-CLS principal survey responses as separate populations of interest, we examined whether their responses were significantly different. However, we did not attribute any significant differences to the cohesion of the sites. A number of district characteristics could be contributing to any observed differences.

There are a number of significant limitations to conducting this kind of analysis. First, we grouped the states and their associated districts into CLS and non-CLS designations, and the resulting sample size was only 10 states. This may not have provided enough statistical power to estimate whether there are statistically significant differences between principal responses across these two groups. Furthermore, what we observe to be differences between CLS and non-CLS states on these principal responses may be the result not of the CLS designation, but rather of a chance grouping of states into the two groups.

To test for this possibility, we conducted a permutation test consisting of three steps. First, a statistical program randomly assigned six states to the CLS category and four states to the non-CLS category. Second, the program tested whether the differences between the principals' mean responses in the CLS and non-CLS categories were statistically significant. The random assignments and means testing occurred more than 200 times. Third, the program calculated the proportion of times the absolute value of the test statistic for the difference between CLS and non-CLS sites, as originally grouped by The Wallace Foundation, was greater than the test statistics of differences from the randomly assigned groupings. This proportion represents the p-value, and we consider 0.05 to be a statistically significant result. That is, the difference between CLS and non-CLS states is not the result of a chance grouping of the principals into these two categories. It is important to note that we account for the state as the primary sampling unit in this case, because the analysis of differences by CLS grouping is a state-level analysis.

Tables F.2 through F.27 document the differences in principal-reported conditions, time spent, and perceptions of the appropriateness of time spent between CLS and non-CLS sites. We report the mean response for principals in the two types of sites, the difference between the means, and the p-value determined by the permutation test.

Table F.2
Difference Between Principals' Responses in CLS and Non-CLS Sites on Data

	CLS Mean	Non-CLS Mean	Mean Difference	p-value
Data Index	1.816 (0.032)	1.887 (0.036)	−0.071	0.714

Survey item: *To what extent do you agree with the following statements about state and district student assessment data?*				
State data are available in a timely manner	1.05 (0.05)	1.58 (0.06)	−0.535	0.433
State data are organized and easily accessible	1.83 (0.05)	1.85 (0.04)	−0.017	0.928
State data are accurate and reliable	1.83 (0.04)	1.88 (0.04)	−0.049	0.995
State data are useful for helping staff improve teaching and learning	2.05 (0.05)	1.98 (0.05)	0.066	0.680
District data are available in a timely manner	1.84 (0.05)	1.83 (0.06)	0.012	0.961
District data are organized and easily accessible	1.93 (0.04)	1.89 (0.05)	0.041	0.861
District data are accurate and reliable	1.89 (0.04)	1.93 (0.05)	−0.041	0.819
District data are useful for helping staff improve teaching and learning	2.07 (0.04)	2.12 (0.05)	−0.050	0.738

NOTES: N = 340 CLS principals, 177 non-CLS principals.
Scale: 0 = strongly disagree; 1 = disagree; 2 = agree; 3 = strongly agree. Standard error shown in parentheses.

Table F.3
Difference Between Principals' Responses in CLS and Non-CLS Sites on Resources

	CLS Mean	Non-CLS Mean	Mean Difference	p-value
Resources Index	1.414 (0.039)	1.249 (0.042)	0.165	0.338

Survey item: *To what extent do you agree with the following statements about resources?*				
I have access to sufficient resources to meet the *academic* needs of my school's students	1.2 (0.05)	1.11 (0.05)	0.116	0.628
I have access to sufficient resources to meet the *social and emotional* needs of my school's students	0.9 (0.05)	0.90 (0.06)	0.064	0.761
This school has adequate facilities and/or transportation	1.9 (0.06)	1.71 (0.05)	0.252	0.109
I have the time and staff support to accomplish all that is required to effectively lead this school	1.5 (0.05)	1.23 (0.05)	0.273	0.090

NOTES: N = 338 CLS principals, 177 non-CLS principals.
Scale: 0 = strongly disagree; 1 = disagree; 2 = agree; 3 = strongly agree.

Table F.4
Difference Between Principals' Responses in CLS and Non-CLS Sites
on Aligned Governance

Aligned-Governance Item	CLS Mean	Non-CLS Mean	Mean Difference	p-value
Survey item: *To what extent do you agree with the following statements about your district's and school's governance structure?*				
Roles and responsibilities of governing entities (e.g., district offices, district board, superintendent's office) are aligned and coordinated	1.956 (0.060)	1.895 (0.064)	0.906	0.728

NOTES: N = 328 CLS principals, 177 non-CLS principals.
Scale: 0 = not at all; 1 = to a small extent; 2 = to a moderate extent; 3 = to a large extent.

Table F.5
Difference Between Principals' Responses in CLS and Non-CLS Sites
on Conflicting Policies

Conflicting-Policies Item	CLS Mean	Non-CLS Mean	Mean Difference	p-value
Survey item: *To what extent does the district or charter management agency provide the following?*				
Policies and programs that are burdensome, conflicting, or fragmented	1.505 (0.057)	1.419 (0.062)	0.085	0.961

NOTES: N = 332 CLS principals, 175 non-CLS principals.
Scale: 0 = not at all; 1 = to a small extent; 2 = to a moderate extent; 3 = to a large extent.

Table F.6
Difference Between Principals' Responses in CLS and Non-CLS Sites on Quality of District Tools, PD, and Evaluation

	CLS Mean	Non-CLS Mean	Mean Difference	p-value
Quality of District Tools, PD, and Evaluation Index	1.883 (0.045)	1.816 (0.048)	0.066	0.723

Survey item: *To what extent does the district or charter management agency provide the following?*

	CLS Mean	Non-CLS Mean	Mean Difference	p-value
Tools and training on using data to inform instructional planning	2.2 (0.05)	2.19 (0.05)	0.013	0.961
High-quality PD opportunities for principals	1.7 (0.05)	1.99 (0.05)	−0.217	0.314
Performance evaluations that are based on state leadership standards	1.9 (0.06)	1.71 (0.07)	0.196	0.476
Performance evaluations that focus on principals' active involvement in instruction	1.9 (0.06)	1.75 (0.06)	0.101	0.690
Performance evaluations that use clear and transparent criteria	1.8 (0.06)	1.69 (0.06)	0.142	0.623
Access to technical assistance in guiding instructional improvements (e.g., coaches, mentors)	1.7 (0.06)	1.54 (0.06)	0.150	0.409

NOTES: N = 336 CLS principals, 177 non-CLS principals.
Scale: 0 = not at all; 1 = to a small extent; 2 = to a moderate extent; 3 = to a large extent.

Table F.7
Difference Between Principals' Responses in CLS and Non-CLS Sites on District-Provision-of-Assistance-with-Administration Item

District-Provision-of-Assistance-with-Administration Item	CLS Mean	Non-CLS Mean	Mean Difference	p-value
Survey item: *To what extent does the district or charter management agency provide the following?*				
Direct assistance with administrative duties so principals can focus on improving instruction (e.g., a school administrative manager or SAM)	0.886 (0.064)	0.763 (0.072)	0.122	0.619

NOTES: N = 336 CLS principals, 175 non-CLS principals.
Scale: 0 = not at all; 1 = to a small extent; 2 = to a moderate extent; 3 = to a large extent.

Table F.8
Difference Between Principals' Responses in CLS and Non-CLS Sites on Sufficient-and-Qualified-Leadership-Staff Item

Sufficient-and-Qualified-Leadership-Staff Item	CLS Mean	Non-CLS Mean	Mean Difference	p-value
Survey item: *To what extent does the district or charter management agency provide the following?*				
Sufficient and qualified leadership staff (e.g., assistant principals, school-based coaches)	1.728 (0.060)	1.466 (0.072)	0.261	0.238

NOTES: N = 333 CLS principals, 175 non-CLS principals.
Scale: 0 = not at all; 1 = to a small extent; 2 = to a moderate extent; 3 = to a large extent.

Table F.9
Difference Between Principals' Responses in CLS and Non-CLS Sites on Autonomy

	CLS Mean	Non-CLS Mean	Mean Difference	p-value
Autonomy Index	1.703 (0.029)	1.252 (0.035)	0.451	0.047
Survey item: *How much decisionmaking authority do you have in the following activities at this school?*				
Setting achievement goals for students	1.93 (0.05)	1.90 (0.06)	0.030	0.780
Determining the daily schedule	2.16 (0.04)	2.14 (0.05)	0.021	0.738
Establishing curriculum	1.45 (0.05)	0.86 (0.05)	0.580	0.038
Selecting textbooks and other instructional materials	1.70 (0.05)	0.90 (0.04)	0.798	0.038
Deciding how the school budget will be spent	1.88 (0.05)	1.86 (0.05)	0.014	0.885
Hiring new full-time teachers	2.18 (0.04)	1.43 (0.06)	0.754	0.161
Determining how to evaluate teachers	1.18 (0.06)	0.96 (0.07)	0.219	0.457
Removing and disciplining teachers	1.43 (0.04)	1.00 (0.05)	0.428	0.014
Hiring new full-time administrators (e.g., assistant principal)	1.86 (0.05)	0.74 (0.06)	1.121	0.133
Removing and disciplining school administrators	1.23 (0.06)	0.61 (0.05)	0.613	0.080

NOTES: N = 337 CLS principals, 179 non-CLS principals.
Scale: 0 = none; 1 = some; 2 = a lot; 3 = complete.

Table F.10
**Difference Between Principals' Reports in CLS and Non-CLS Sites
on Time Spent Building a Common Vision**

	CLS Mean	Non-CLS Mean	Mean Difference	p-value
Time Spent Building a Common Vision Index	0.478 (0.028)	0.454 (0.031)	0.024	0.900
Survey item: *How much time and effort did you spend on the following?*				
Developing, implementing, and monitoring strategic goals for this school	0.55 (0.03)	0.54 (0.04)	0.009	0.909
Assisting staff in developing a shared vision of our mission and goals	0.52 (0.03)	0.51 (0.04)	0.116	0.923
Involving parents in supporting the strategic goals of this school	0.34 (0.03)	0.31 (0.04)	0.038	0.833

NOTES: N = 326 CLS principals, 176 non-CLS principals.
Scale: 0 = no time or some time and effort; 1 = a great deal of time and effort.

Table F.11
**Difference Between Principals' Reports in CLS and Non-CLS Sites
on Appropriateness of Time Spent Building a Common Vision**

	CLS Mean	Non-CLS Mean	Mean Difference	p-value
Appropriateness of Time Spent Building a Common Vision Index	0.683 (0.028)	0.630 (0.029)	0.052	0.495
Survey item: *How do you feel about the time and effort you spend on the following?*				
Developing, implementing, and monitoring strategic goals for this school	0.74 (0.03)	0.68 (0.04)	0.062	0.485
Assisting staff in developing a shared vision of our mission and goals	0.73 (0.03)	0.67 (0.04)	0.060	0.376
Involving parents in supporting the strategic goals of this school	0.57 (0.03)	0.53 (0.04)	0.033	0.695

NOTES: N = 326 CLS principals, 176 non-CLS principals.
Scale: 0 = insufficient or excessive for this school; 1 = appropriate and sufficient.

Table F.12
Difference Between Principals' Reports in CLS and Non-CLS Sites on Time Spent on School Improvement Efforts

	CLS Mean	Non-CLS Mean	Mean Difference	p-value
School Improvement Efforts Index	0.644 (0.024)	0.491 (0.028)	0.153	0.061
Survey item: How much time and effort did you spend on the following?				
Aligning human and fiscal resources to strategic priorities	0.68 (0.03)	0.49 (0.03)	0.196	0.033
Monitoring the phase-in of school improvement efforts and their impact on student learning	0.56 (0.03)	0.39 (0.03)	0.172	0.194
Using data to monitor school progress, identify problems, and propose solutions	0.67 (0.03)	0.58 (0.03)	0.085	0.276

NOTES: N = 326 CLS principals, 175 non-CLS principals.
Scale: 0 = no time or some time and effort; 1 = a great deal of time and effort.

Table F.13
Difference Between Principals' Reports in CLS and Non-CLS Sites on Appropriateness of Time Spent on School Improvement Efforts

	CLS Mean	Non-CLS Mean	Mean Difference	p-value
Appropriateness of Time Spent on School Improvement Efforts Index	0.773 (0.021)	0.677 (0.027)	0.095	0.023
Survey item: How do you feel about the time and effort you spend on the following?				
Aligning human and fiscal resources to strategic priorities	0.83* (0.02)	0.73 (0.03)	0.094	0.038
Monitoring the phase-in of school improvement efforts and their impact on student learning	0.75 (0.02)	0.66 (0.03)	0.095	0.057
Using data to monitor school progress, identify problems, and propose solutions	0.73 (0.03)	0.64 (0.03)	0.091	0.085

NOTES: N = 326 CLS principals, 175 non-CLS principals.
Scale: 0 = insufficient or excessive for this school; 1 = appropriate and sufficient.

Table F.14
Difference Between Principals' Reports in CLS and Non-CLS Sites on Time Spent Creating a Supportive Learning Environment for Students

	CLS Mean	Non-CLS Mean	Mean Difference	p-value
Supportive Learning Environment Index	0.755 (0.537)	0.690 (0.029)	0.064	0.452
Survey item: How much time and effort did you spend on the following?				
Ensuring that disruptions of instructional time are minimized	0.73 (0.02)	0.62 (0.03)	0.105	0.328
Establishing a safe and orderly environment	0.77 (0.02)	0.75 (0.03)	0.024	0.652

NOTES: N = 327 CLS principals, 175 non-CLS principals.
Scale: 0 = no time or some time and effort; 1 = a great deal of time and effort.

Table F.15
Difference Between Principals' Reports in CLS and Non-CLS Sites on Appropriateness of Time Spent Creating a Supportive Learning Environment for Students

	CLS Mean	Non-CLS Mean	Mean Difference	p-value
Supportive Learning Environment Index	0.773 (0.021)	0.677 (0.027)	0.095	0.023
Survey item: How do you feel about the time and effort you spend on the following?				
Ensuring that disruptions of instructional time are minimized	0.75 (0.03)	0.78 (0.03)	−0.027	0.447
Establishing a safe and orderly environment	0.79 (0.02)	0.76 (0.03)	0.034	0.361

NOTES: N = 327 CLS principals, 175 non-CLS principals.
Scale: 0 = insufficient or excessive for this school; 1 = appropriate and sufficient.

Table F.16
Difference Between Principals' Reports in CLS and Non-CLS Sites on Time Spent Motivating Students

	CLS Mean	Non-CLS Mean	Mean Difference	p-value
Motivating Students Index	0.583 (0.025)	0.490 (0.028)	0.092	0.371
Survey item: How much time and effort did you spend on the following?				
Acknowledging students for academic effort and/or achievement	0.56 (0.03)	0.47 (0.03)	0.093	0.338
Communicating high expectations to students	0.77 (0.02)	0.49 (0.03)	0.085	0.071
Providing incentives for students to improve their learning	0.41 (0.03)	0.31 (0.03)	0.097	0.671

NOTES: N = 327 CLS principals, 175 non-CLS principals.
Scale: 0 = no time or some time and effort; 1 = a great deal of time and effort.

Table F.17
Difference Between Principals' Reports in CLS and Non-CLS Sites on Appropriateness of Time Spent Motivating Students

	CLS Mean	Non-CLS Mean	Mean Difference	p-value
Motivating Students Index	0.761 (0.023)	0.658 (0.031)	0.102	0.023
Survey item: How do you feel about the time and effort you spend on the following?				
Acknowledging students for academic effort and/or achievement	0.78 (0.02)	0.66 (0.03)	0.118	0.047
Communicating high expectations to students	0.77 (0.02)	0.68 (0.03)	0.094	0.038
Providing incentives for students to improve their learning	0.72 (0.03)	0.62 (0.03)	0.102	0.071

NOTES: N = 327 CLS principals, 175 non-CLS principals.
Scale: 0 = insufficient or excessive for this school; 1 = appropriate and sufficient.

Table F.18
Difference Between Principals' Reports in CLS and Non-CLS Sites on Time Spent Monitoring Classroom Instruction

	CLS Mean	Non-CLS Mean	Mean Difference	p-value
Monitoring Classroom Instruction Index	0.305 (0.023)	0.234 (0.026)	0.071	0.328
Survey item: *How much time and effort did you spend on the following?*				
Collecting and examining student work	0.28 (0.03)	0.24 (0.03)	0.032	0.609
Organizing walkthroughs or classroom visits in order to gather information	0.40 (0.03)	0.27 (0.03)	0.130	0.285
Reviewing and providing feedback on teacher lesson plans	0.22 (0.02)	0.18 (0.03)	0.047	0.542

NOTES: N = 325 CLS principals, 176 non-CLS principals.
Scale: 0 = no time or some time and effort; 1 = a great deal of time and effort.

Table F.19
Difference Between Principals' Reports in CLS and Non-CLS Sites on Appropriateness of Time Spent Monitoring Classroom Instruction

	CLS Mean	Non-CLS Mean	Mean Difference	p-value
Monitoring Classroom Instruction Index	0.589 (0.027)	0.446 (0.030)	0.143	0.052
Survey item: *How do you feel about the time and effort you spend on the following?*				
Collecting and examining student work	0.54 (0.03)	0.44 (0.03)	0.097	0.285
Organizing walkthroughs or classroom visits in order to gather information	0.64 (0.03)	0.45 (0.03)	0.189	0.066
Reviewing and providing feedback on teacher lesson plans	0.57 (0.03)	0.43 (0.03)	0.143	0.119

NOTES: N = 325 CLS principals, 176 non-CLS principals.
Scale: 0 = insufficient or excessive for this school; 1 = appropriate and sufficient.

Table F.20
Difference Between Principals' Reports in CLS and Non-CLS Sites on Time Spent Engaging Teachers Outside of the Classroom

	CLS Mean	Non-CLS Mean	Mean Difference	p-value
Engaging with Teachers Outside of the Classroom to Improve the Instruction of Students Index	0.77 (0.02)	0.71 (0.03)	0.062	0.076
Survey item: *How much time and effort did you spend on the following?*				
Creating opportunities for staff collaboration with a focus on improving student achievement	0.57 (0.03)	0.37 (0.03)	0.198	0.109
Holding teachers accountable for student academic progress	0.63 (0.03)	0.48 (0.03)	0.144	0.085
Setting up systems for teachers to examine student work in relation to grade-level expectations and/or state standards	0.51 (0.03)	0.39 (0.03)	0.117	0.161
Guiding the development and evaluation of curriculum that is aligned with local and state standards and assessments	0.43 (0.03)	0.26 (0.03)	0.167	0.109

NOTES: N = 327 CLS principals, 176 non-CLS principals.
Scale: 0 = no time or some time and effort; 1 = a great deal of time and effort.

Table F.21
Difference Between Principals' Reports in CLS and Non-CLS Sites on Appropriateness of Time Spent Engaging Teachers Outside of the Classroom

	CLS Mean	Non-CLS Mean	Mean Difference	p-value
Engaging with Teachers Outside of the Classroom to Improve the Instruction of Students Index	0.78 (0.02)	0.66 (0.03)	0.116	0.023
Survey item: *How much time and effort did you spend on the following?*				
Creating opportunities for staff collaboration with a focus on improving student achievement	0.67 (0.03)	0.53 (0.03)	0.134	0.004
Holding teachers accountable for student academic progress	0.83 (0.02)	0.75 (0.03)	0.072	0.138
Setting up systems for teachers to examine student work in relation to grade-level expectations and/or state standards	0.69 (0.03)	0.61 (0.03)	0.077	0.03
Guiding the development and evaluation of curriculum that is aligned with local and state standards and assessments	0.75 (0.02)	0.67 (0.03)	0.076	0.185

NOTES: N = 327 CLS principals, 176 non-CLS principals.
Scale: 0 = insufficient or excessive for this school; 1 = appropriate and sufficient.

Table F.22
Difference Between Principals' Reports in CLS and Non-CLS Sites on Time Spent Promoting Staff PD

	CLS Mean	Non-CLS Mean	Mean Difference	p-value
Promoting Staff PD Index	0.465 (0.025)	0.395 (0.026)	0.070	0.290
Survey item: How much time and effort did you spend on the following?				
Working with teachers and other staff to help them use achievement data from the state, district, or school level for their decisionmaking	0.60 (0.03)	0.48 (0.03)	0.118	0.271
Arranging high-quality PD experiences for teachers and staff in areas known to improve student achievement	0.57 (0.03)	0.46 (0.03)	0.115	0.100
Helping staff members find resources to accomplish their professional goals	0.33 (0.03)	0.28 (0.03)	0.047	0.657
Working with individual staff members to evaluate their particular professional needs and capacities	0.33 (0.03)	0.35 (0.03)	−0.020	0.752

NOTES: N = 326 CLS principals, 176 non-CLS principals.
Scale: 0 = no time or some time and effort; 1 = a great deal of time and effort.

Table F.23
Difference Between Principals' Reports in CLS and Non-CLS Sites on Appropriateness of Time Spent Promoting Staff PD

	CLS Mean	Non-CLS Mean	Mean Difference	p-value
Promoting Staff PD Index	0.709 (0.025)	0.622 (0.026)	0.087	0.038
Survey item: How do you feel about the time and effort you spend on the following?				
Working with teachers and other staff to help them use achievement data from the state, district, or school level for their decisionmaking	0.69 (0.03)	0.59 (0.03)	0.093	0.104
Arranging high-quality PD experiences for teachers and staff in areas known to improve student achievement	0.75 (0.03)	0.65 (0.03)	0.099	0.047
Helping staff members find resources to accomplish their professional goals	0.72 (0.03)	0.67 (0.03)	0.051	0.166
Working with individual staff members to evaluate their particular professional needs and capacities	0.68 (0.03)	0.57 (0.03)	0.111	0.042

NOTES: N = 326 CLS principals, 176 non-CLS principals.
Scale: 0 = insufficient or excessive for this school; 1 = appropriate and sufficient.

Table F.24
Difference Between Principals' Reports in CLS and Non-CLS Sites on Time Spent Motivating Staff

	CLS Mean	Non-CLS Mean	Mean Difference	p-value
Motivating Staff Index	0.448 (0.026)	0.351 (0.026)	0.097	0.147
Survey item: *How much time and effort did you spend on the following?*				
Acknowledging exceptional staff effort and/or performance	0.35 (0.03)	0.23 (0.03)	0.124	0.190
Communicating high expectations for staff	0.64 (0.03)	0.53 (0.03)	0.109	0.247
Stimulating staff to consider how they could carry out their work more effectively	0.34 (0.03)	0.28 (0.03)	0.053	0.414

NOTES: N = 325 CLS principals, 176 non-CLS principals.
Scale: 0 = no time or some time and effort; 1 = a great deal of time and effort.

Table F.25
Difference Between Principals' Reports in CLS and Non-CLS Sites on Appropriateness of Time Spent Motivating Staff

	CLS Mean	Non-CLS Mean	Mean Difference	p-value
Motivating Staff Index	0.724 (0.023)	0.617 (0.028)	0.107	0.000
Survey item: *How do you feel about the time and effort you spend on the following?*				
Acknowledging exceptional staff effort and/or performance	0.69 (0.03)	0.56 (0.03)	0.130	0.028
Communicating high expectations for staff	0.77 (0.02)	0.70 (0.03)	0.068	0.142
Stimulating staff to consider how they could carry out their work more effectively	0.70* (0.03)	0.57 (0.03)	0.127	0.019

NOTES: N = 325 CLS principals, 176 non-CLS principals.
Scale: 0 = insufficient or excessive for this school; 1 = appropriate and sufficient.

Table F.26
**Difference Between Principals' Reports in CLS and Non-CLS Sites
on Time Spent Fostering Leadership Among Staff**

	CLS Mean	Non-CLS Mean	Mean Difference	p-value
Fostering Leadership Among Staff Index	0.555 (0.030)	0.413 (0.033)	0.142	0.004
Survey item: *How much time and effort did you spend on the following?*				
Developing leadership capacity of staff	0.50 (0.03)	0.36 (0.03)	0.147	0.028
Encouraging individual, small-team, and whole-school problem-solving	0.61 (0.03)	0.49 (0.03)	0.122	0.004
Establishing and developing school leadership teams	0.53 (0.03)	0.38 (0.03)	0.149	0.004

NOTES: N = 325 CLS principals, 176 non-CLS principals.
Scale: 0 = no time or some time and effort; 1 = a great deal of time and effort.

Table F.27
**Difference Between Principals' Reports in CLS and Non-CLS Sites on Appropriateness of
Time Spent Fostering Leadership Among Staff**

	CLS Mean	Non-CLS Mean	Mean Difference	p-value
Fostering Leadership Among Staff Index	0.793 (0.022)	0.717 (0.029)	0.076	0.276
Survey item: *How do you feel about the time and effort you spend on the following?*				
Developing leadership capacity of staff	0.80 (0.02)	0.71 (0.03)	0.074	0.385
Encouraging individual, small-team, and whole-school problem-solving	0.78 (0.02)	0.69 (0.03)	0.092	0.228
Establishing and developing school leadership teams	0.78 (0.02)	0.72 (0.03)	0.064	0.238

NOTES: N = 325 CLS principals, 176 non-CLS principals.
Scale: 0 = insufficient or excessive for this school; 1 = appropriate and sufficient.

Mapping the Relationships Between Conditions and Instructional Leadership Practices

In this section, we discuss the methodology we used to examine the relationship between principal-reported conditions and time spent and perceptions of the appropriateness of time spent on instructional leadership practices.

We used OLS, factoring in the complex survey design and the clustered nature of the data. We modeled each index of time spent and perceptions of time spent as the dependent variable and each condition index or item as the independent variable. We included the school-level control variables described earlier in this appendix (reading proficiency, percentage of economically disadvantaged students, student enrollment, percentage of African-American enrollment, a school-level indicator, the principal's years of experience in the school) and an indicator for each district to control for district-level effects.

The model is the following:

$$Y = \alpha + \beta_1 C + \beta_2 R + \beta_3 ED + \beta_4 EN + \beta_5 A + \beta_6 HS + \beta_6 M + \beta_7 P + \beta_8 EX + \beta_9 D + \varepsilon \qquad (1)$$

where

Y = index of principal's report of time spent on instructional leadership or that time spent was appropriate

α = intercept

C = index of principal's report of any given condition

R = proportion of students in a principal's school achieving proficient or better on the state's reading or English language arts student assessment

ED = percentage of students in the school who are economically disadvantaged (eligible to receive free or reduced-price lunch)

EN = total student enrollment at the school

A = percentage of students in the school who are African-American

HS = a dummy variable that indicates whether the school is a high school (grades 9–12)

M = a dummy variable that indicates whether the school is a middle school (grades 6–8)

P = a dummy variable that indicates whether the school is a primary school (grades K–5)

EX = years of experience of the principal at the school

D = dummy variable for each study district

ε = unmeasured error

For these models, we used the nonresponse weights calculated for the entire sample of principals (principals from all states included in the study as the population of interest), specifying the principal as the primary sampling unit and the school district as the stratum.

Tables F.28 through F.43 report standardized coefficients that are estimated after converting all the dependent and independent variables into having a mean of 0 and standard deviation of 1. We used the *listcoef* command in Stata developed by Long and Freese (2005) to calculate these coefficients. We can compare the standardized coefficients with each other to determine the relative magnitude of the relationship between a condition and an instructional leadership practice. The closer the coefficients are to

1.0, the stronger the relationship is between the condition and an instructional leadership practice. The results are organized by condition. We first present results on time spent on instructional leadership practices and then present results on perceptions of time spent.

Table F.28
OLS Regression Results for Data Index on Time Spent

Data Index	Coefficient	t-statistic	p-value	Standardized Coefficient
Building a common vision	0.182 (0.049)	3.72	0.000	0.233
School improvement efforts	0.097 (0.046)	2.10	0.036	0.144
Supportive learning environment	0.032 (0.044)	0.72	0.472	0.046
Motivating students	0.095 (0.046)	2.08	0.038	0.137
Monitoring classroom instruction	0.138 (0.039)	3.51	0.000	0.215
Engaging with teachers outside of the classroom	0.090 (0.042)	2.15	0.032	0.142
Promoting staff PD	0.094 (0.042)	2.23	0.026	0.141
Motivating staff	0.114 (0.045)	2.52	0.012	0.166
Developing leadership teams	0.008 (0.052)	0.16	0.876	0.009

NOTE: N = 598; standard error shown in parentheses.

Table F.29
OLS Regression Results for Resources Index on Time Spent

Resources Index	Coefficient	t-statistic	p-value	Standardized Coefficient
Building a common vision	0.065 (0.039)	1.65	0.099	0.097
School improvement efforts	0.095 (0.032)	2.96	0.003	0.166
Supportive learning environment	0.013 (0.032)	0.41	0.684	0.022
Motivating students	0.060 (0.034)	1.75	0.080	0.101
Monitoring classroom instruction	0.153 (0.030)	5.05	0.000	0.279
Engaging with teachers outside of the classroom	0.065 (0.029)	2.19	0.029	0.119
Promoting staff PD	0.121 (0.031)	3.87	0.000	0.212
Motivating staff	0.101 (0.035)	2.88	0.004	0.172
Developing leadership teams	0.046 (0.040)	1.16	0.247	0.066

NOTE: N = 598; standard error shown in parentheses.

Table F.30
OLS Regression Results for Aligned-Governance Item on Time Spent

Aligned-Governance Item	Coefficient	t-statistic	p-value	Standardized Coefficient
Building a common vision	0.050 (0.026)	1.95	0.052	0.108
School improvement efforts	0.057 (0.021)	2.69	0.007	0.142
Supportive learning environment	0.013 (0.023)	0.56	0.574	0.032
Motivating students	0.063 (0.021)	2.89	0.004	0.152
Monitoring classroom instruction	0.087 (0.019)	4.47	0.000	0.228
Engaging with teachers outside of the classroom	0.058 (0.019)	2.95	0.003	0.153
Promoting staff PD	0.069 (0.023)	3.00	0.003	0.174
Motivating staff	0.056 (0.023)	2.39	0.017	0.136
Developing leadership teams	0.022 (0.029)	0.75	0.455	0.045

NOTE: N = 598; standard error shown in parentheses.

Table F.31
OLS Regression Results for Conflicting-Policies Item on Time Spent

Conflicting-Policies Item	Coefficient	t-statistic	p-value	Standardized coefficient
Building a common vision	−0.032 (0.026)	−1.21	0.227	−0.066
School improvement efforts	−0.022 (0.022)	−1.02	0.310	−0.054
Supportive learning environment	0.032 (0.022)	1.40	0.161	0.074
Motivating students	−0.001 (0.023)	−0.05	0.963	−0.002
Monitoring classroom instruction	0.010 (0.022)	0.47	0.641	0.027
Engaging with teachers outside of the classroom	−0.018 (0.021)	−0.85	0.396	−0.046
Promoting staff PD	0.013 (0.023)	0.58	0.565	0.033
Motivating staff	0.017 (0.024)	0.72	0.469	0.042
Developing leadership teams	−0.003 (0.028)	−0.11	0.912	−0.006

NOTE: N = 598; standard error shown in parentheses.

Table F.32
OLS Regression Results for Quality-of-District-Provided-Tools,-PD,-and-Evaluation Item on Time Spent

Quality-of-District-Provided-Tools,-PD,-and-Evaluation Item	Coefficient	t-statistic	p-value	Standardized Coefficient
Building a common vision	0.170 (0.036)	4.36	0.000	0.283
School improvement efforts	0.124 (0.029)	4.24	0.000	0.239
Supportive learning environment	0.060 (0.035)	1.70	0.089	0.112
Motivating students	0.136 (0.033)	4.04	0.000	0.253
Monitoring classroom instruction	0.176 (0.024)	7.20	0.000	0.356
Engaging with teachers outside of the classroom	0.160 (0.025)	6.22	0.000	0.326
Promoting staff PD	0.142 (0.030)	4.66	0.000	0.276
Motivating staff	0.163 (0.030)	5.30	0.000	0.306
Developing leadership teams	0.070 (0.039)	1.80	0.073	0.111

NOTE: N = 598; standard error shown in parentheses.

Table F.33
OLS Regression Results for District-Provides-Administrative-Assistance Item on Time Spent

District-Provides-Assistance-with-Administrative-Duties (e.g., SAM) Item	Coefficient	t-statistic	p-value	Standardized Coefficient
Building a common vision	0.073 (0.024)	2.98	0.003	0.174
School improvement efforts	0.037 (0.019)	1.95	0.052	0.103
Supportive learning environment	−0.033 (0.020)	−1.67	0.096	−0.089
Motivating students	0.016 (0.020)	0.79	0.430	0.042
Monitoring classroom instruction	0.088 (0.021)	4.07	0.000	0.254
Engaging with teachers outside of the classroom	0.040 (0.018)	2.16	0.031	0.116
Promoting staff PD	0.057 (0.022)	2.60	0.010	0.160
Motivating staff	0.085 (0.021)	3.92	0.000	0.228
Developing leadership teams	−0.022 (0.025)	−0.87	0.387	−0.049

NOTE: N = 598; standard error shown in parentheses.

Table F.34
OLS Regression Results for District-Provides-Sufficient-and-Qualified-Leadership-Staff Item on Time Spent

District-Provides-Sufficient-and-Qualified Leadership-Staff (e.g., Assistant Principals, school-based coaches) Item	Coefficient	t-statistic	p-value	Standardized Coefficient
Building a common vision	0.049 (0.027)	1.82	0.070	0.109
School improvement efforts	0.047 (0.021)	2.17	0.031	0.120
Supportive learning environment	−0.008 (0.020)	−0.39	0.697	−0.019
Motivating students	0.038 (0.020)	1.82	0.069	0.095
Monitoring classroom instruction	0.064 (0.022)	2.84	0.005	0.173
Engaging with teachers outside of the classroom	0.046 (0.020)	2.32	0.021	0.126
Promoting staff PD	0.067 (0.023)	2.90	0.004	0.174
Motivating staff	0.066 (0.024)	2.69	0.007	0.165
Developing leadership teams	0.028 (0.028)	1.02	0.308	0.061

NOTE: N = 598; standard error shown in parentheses.

Table F.35
OLS Regression Results for Autonomy Index on Time Spent

Autonomy Index	Coefficient	t-statistic	p-value	Standardized Coefficient
Building a common vision	0.101 (0.052)	1.94	0.052	0.125
School improvement efforts	0.159 (0.043)	3.66	0.000	0.230
Supportive learning environment	0.099 (0.045)	2.16	0.031	0.137
Motivating students	0.088 (0.046)	1.89	0.060	0.123
Monitoring classroom instruction	0.181 (0.042)	4.23	0.000	0.274
Engaging with teachers outside of the classroom	0.192 (0.037)	5.17	0.000	0.292
Promoting staff PD	0.267 (0.039)	6.84	0.000	0.389
Motivating staff	0.221 (0.044)	5.03	0.000	0.310
Developing leadership teams	0.142 (0.058)	2.45	0.015	0.168

NOTE: N = 598; standard error shown in parentheses.

Table F.36
OLS Regression Results for Data Index on Appropriateness of Time Spent

Data Index	Coefficient	t-statistic	p-value	Standardized Coefficient
Building a common vision	0.065 (0.041)	1.58	0.116	0.089
School improvement efforts	0.087 (0.033)	2.60	0.010	0.141
Supportive learning environment	0.064 (0.037)	1.70	0.090	0.095
Motivating students	0.089 (0.039)	2.29	0.022	0.134
Monitoring classroom instruction	0.124 (0.042)	2.96	0.003	0.164
Engaging with teachers outside of the classroom	0.059 (0.033)	1.81	0.071	0.100
Promoting staff PD	0.079 (0.037)	2.10	0.036	0.118
Motivating staff	0.109 (0.034)	3.19	0.002	0.161
Developing leadership teams	0.045 (0.034)	1.33	0.183	0.067

NOTE: N = 598; standard error shown in parentheses.

Table F.37
OLS Regression Results for Resources Index on Appropriateness of Time Spent

Resources Index	Coefficient	t-statistic	p-value	Standardized Coefficient
Building a common vision	0.147 (0.035)	4.22	0.000	0.236
School improvement efforts	0.127 (0.027)	4.64	0.000	0.243
Supportive learning environment	0.080 (0.034)	2.30	0.022	0.139
Motivating students	0.096 (0.032)	2.96	0.003	0.169
Monitoring classroom instruction	0.181 (0.033)	5.44	0.000	0.280
Engaging with teachers outside of the classroom	0.112 (0.027)	4.13	0.000	0.221
Promoting staff PD	0.196 (0.030)	6.34	0.000	0.343
Motivating staff	0.157 (0.028)	5.51	0.000	0.271
Developing leadership teams	0.085 (0.031)	2.73	0.007	0.147

NOTE: N = 598; standard error shown in parentheses.

Table F.38
OLS Regression Results for Aligned-Governance Item on Appropriateness of Time Spent

Aligned-Governance Item	Coefficient	t-statistic	p-value	Standardized Coefficient
Building a common vision	0.075 (0.020)	3.63	0.000	0.173
School improvement efforts	0.028 (0.021)	1.34	0.181	0.077
Supportive learning environment	0.013 (0.026)	0.51	0.609	0.033
Motivating students	0.021 (0.023)	0.92	0.359	0.053
Monitoring classroom instruction	0.030 (0.027)	1.10	0.271	0.067
Engaging with teachers outside of the classroom	0.008 (0.019)	0.43	0.665	0.023
Promoting staff PD	0.042 (0.024)	1.73	0.084	0.106
Motivating staff	0.041 (0.022)	1.80	0.073	0.101
Developing leadership teams	0.046 (0.023)	1.94	0.052	0.113

NOTE: N = 598; standard error shown in parentheses.

Table F.39
OLS Regression Results for Conflicting-Policies Item on Appropriateness of Time Spent

Conflicting-Policies Item	Coefficient	t-statistic	p-value	Standardized Coefficient
Building a common vision	−0.028 (0.023)	−1.23	0.218	−0.063
School improvement efforts	−0.021 (0.021)	−1.03	0.306	−0.057
Supportive learning environment	−0.031 (0.022)	−1.40	0.162	−0.076
Motivating students	−0.025 (0.023)	−1.11	0.268	−0.062
Monitoring classroom instruction	−0.022 (0.025)	−0.90	0.366	−0.048
Engaging with teachers outside of the classroom	−0.031 (0.020)	−1.55	0.122	−0.086
Promoting staff PD	−0.023 (0.021)	−1.07	0.285	−0.056
Motivating staff	−0.019 (0.021)	−0.92	0.361	−0.046
Developing leadership teams	−0.064 (0.023)	−2.81	0.005	−0.154

NOTE: N = 598; standard error shown in parentheses.

Table F.40
OLS Regression Results for District-Provided-Tools,-PD,-and-Evaluation Item on Appropriateness of Time Spent

Quality-of-District-Provided-Tools,-PD,-and-Evaluation Item	Coefficient	t-statistic	p-value	Standardized Coefficient
Building a common vision	0.084 (0.033)	2.50	0.013	0.149
School improvement efforts	0.058 (0.028)	2.03	0.043	0.122
Supportive learning environment	−0.010 (0.029)	−0.37	0.715	−0.020
Motivating students	0.068 (0.028)	2.36	0.018	0.132
Monitoring classroom instruction	0.103 (0.035)	2.95	0.003	0.177
Engaging with teachers outside of the classroom	0.023 (0.027)	0.85	0.397	0.050
Promoting staff PD	0.083 (0.032)	2.57	0.010	0.162
Motivating staff	0.079 (0.030)	2.61	0.009	0.152
Developing leadership teams	0.067 (0.029)	2.26	0.024	0.129

NOTE: N = 598; standard error shown in parentheses.

Table F.41
OLS Regression Results for District-Provides-Administrative-Assistance Item on Appropriateness of Time Spent

District-Provides-Assistance-with-Administrative-Duties (e.g., SAM) Item	Coefficient	t-statistic	p-value	Standardized Coefficient
Building a common vision	0.068 (0.022)	3.02	0.003	0.172
School improvement efforts	0.010 (0.020)	0.50	0.620	0.031
Supportive learning environment	0.005 (0.020)	0.29	0.770	0.016
Motivating students	0.005 (0.020)	0.25	0.805	0.013
Monitoring classroom instruction	0.063 (0.023)	2.73	0.007	0.155
Engaging with teachers outside of the classroom	0.000 (0.020)	0.04	0.969	0.002
Promoting staff PD	0.019 (0.022)	0.87	0.385	0.053
Motivating staff	0.009 (0.022)	0.40	0.689	0.025
Developing leadership teams	−0.015 (0.022)	−0.68	0.499	−0.041

NOTE: N = 598; standard error shown in parentheses.

Table F.42
OLS Regression Results for District-Provides-Sufficient-and-Qualified-Leadership-Staff Item on Appropriateness of Time Spent

District-Provides-Sufficient-and-Qualified-Leadership-Staff (e.g., assistant principals, school-based coaches) Item	Coefficient	t-statistic	p-value	Standardized Coefficient
Building a common vision	0.056 (0.026)	2.16	0.031	0.134
School improvement efforts	0.030 (0.020)	1.47	0.142	0.085
Supportive learning environment	−0.003 (0.021)	−0.17	0.865	−0.009
Motivating students	0.017 (0.020)	0.85	0.393	0.045
Monitoring classroom instruction	0.055 (0.024)	2.26	0.024	0.127
Engaging with teachers outside of the classroom	0.000 (0.021)	0.04	0.965	0.002
Promoting staff PD	0.044 (0.023)	1.88	0.061	0.117
Motivating staff	0.041 (0.022)	1.83	0.068	0.104
Developing leadership teams	0.028 (0.021)	1.33	0.186	0.075

NOTE: N = 598; standard error shown in parentheses.

Table F.43
OLS Regression Results for Autonomy Index on Appropriateness of Time Spent

Autonomy Index	Coefficient	t-statistic	p-value	Standardized Coefficient
Building a common vision	0.156 (0.046)	3.40	0.001	0.207
School improvement efforts	0.069 (0.043)	1.58	0.115	0.108
Supportive learning environment	−0.085 (0.050)	−1.70	0.089	−0.123
Motivating students	0.062 (0.043)	1.42	0.155	0.090
Monitoring classroom instruction	0.123 (0.057)	2.16	0.031	0.158
Engaging with teachers outside of the classroom	0.016 (0.043)	0.38	0.705	0.027
Promoting staff PD	0.065 (0.049)	1.31	0.190	0.094
Motivating staff	0.093 (0.051)	1.83	0.068	0.134
Developing leadership teams	0.152 (0.040)	3.73	0.000	0.217

NOTE: N = 598; standard error shown in parentheses.

References

Bardach, Eugene, *Getting Agencies to Work Together: The Practice and Theory of Managerial Craftsmanship*, Washington, D.C.: Brookings, 1998.

———, "Developmental Dynamics: Interagency Collaboration as an Emergent Phenomenon," *Journal of Public Administration Research and Theory*, Vol. 11, No. 2, April 2001, pp. 149–164. As of October 18, 2009:
http://jpart.oxfordjournals.org/cgi/reprint/11/2/149

Blase, Rebajo R., and Joseph J. Blase, *Handbook of Instructional Leadership: How Successful Principals Promote Teaching and Learning*, Thousand Oaks, Calif.: Corwin Press, 2004.

Bolman, Lee G., and Terrence E. Deal, *Reframing Organizations: Artistry, Choice, and Leadership*, Hoboken, N.J.: John Wiley and Sons, 2003.

Brewer, Dominic J., "Principal and Student Outcomes: Evidence from U.S. High Schools," *Economics of Education Review*, Vol. 12, No. 4, December 1993, pp. 281–292.

Bryk, Anthony S., Penny B. Bebring, David Kerbow, Sharon Rollow, and John Q. Easton, *Charting Chicago School Reform: Democratic Localism as a Lever for Change*, Boulder, Colo.: Westview Press, 1998.

Bryson, John M., Barbara C. Crosby, and Melissa Middleton Stone, "The Design and Implementation of Cross-Sector Collaborations: Propositions from the Literature," *Public Administration Review*, Vol. 66, Special Issue, December 2006, pp. 44–55.

Coffin, G. A., "The Impact of District Conditions on Principals' Experientially Acquired Professional Learning," Doctoral dissertation, University of Toronto, Canada, *Dissertation Abstracts International*, Vol. 59, No. 6, 1997, p. 1844.

Copland, M. A., "Problem-Based Learning, Problem-Framing Ability and the Principal Selves of Prospective School Principals," Doctoral dissertation, Stanford University, *Dissertation Abstracts International*, Vol. 60, No. 8, 1999, p. 2750.

Council of Chief State School Officers (CCSSO), *Interstate School Leaders Licensure Consortium: Standards for School Leaders*, Washington, D.C.: Council of Chief State School Officers, 1996. As of October 18, 2009:
http://www.ccsso.org/content/pdfs/isllcstd.pdf

Council of Chief State School Officers State Education Center, *School Data Direct*, 2009. As of October 18, 2009:
http://www.schooldatadirect.org

Crews, Alton C., and Sonya Weakley, *Making Leadership Happen: The SREB Model for Leadership Development*, Southern Regional Education Board (SREB) Leadership Preparation Program, 1996. As of October 18, 2009:
http://www.sreb.org/main/Leadership/pubs/TableOfContents.asp

Darling-Hammond, Linda, Michelle LaPointe, Debra Meyerson, and Margaret Terry Orr, *Preparing School Leaders for a Changing World: Lessons from Exemplary Leadership Development Programs: Final Report*, Stanford, Calif.: Stanford University, Stanford Educational Leadership Institute, April 2007. As of October 18, 2009:
http://www.srnleads.org/data/pdfs/sls/sls_tech_report.pdf

Davis, Stephen, Linda Darling-Hammond, Michelle LaPointe, and Debra Meyerson, *School Leadership Study: Developing Successful Principals* (Review of Research), Stanford, Calif.: Stanford University, Stanford Educational Leadership Institute, 2005.

Eberts, Randall W., and Joe A. Stone, "Student Achievement in Public Schools: Do Principals Make a Difference?" *Economics of Education Review*, Vol. 7, No. 3, 1988, pp. 291–299.

Education Commission of the States, *State Constitutions and Public Education Governance*, Denver, Colo.: Education Commission of the States, updated October 2000. As of October 18, 2009:
http://www.ecs.org/clearinghouse/17/03/1703.htm

Elmore, Richard F., *Building a New Structure for School Leadership*, Washington, D.C.: Albert Shanker Institute, 2000.

Fink, Elaine, and Lauren B. Resnick, "Developing Principals as Instructional Leaders," *Phi Delta Kappan*, Vol. 82, No. 8, 2001, pp. 598–606.

Fuhrman, Susan H. (ed.), *Designing Coherent Education Policy: Improving the System*, San Francisco, Calif.: Jossey-Bass Publishers, 1993.

Fuhrman, Susan H., Margaret E. Goertz, and Elliot H. Weinbaum, "Educational Governance in the United States: Where Are We? How Did We Get Here? Why Should We Care? In Susan H. Fuhrman, David K. Cohen, and Fritz Mosher (eds.), *The State of Education Policy Research*, London: Taylor & Francis, 2007.

Fuller, Bruce, Susanna Loeb, Nicole Arshan, Allison Chen, and Susanna Yi, *California Principals' Resources: Acquisition, Deployment and Barriers*, Policy Analysis for California Education (PACE), 2007. As of October 18, 2009:
http://pace.berkeley.edu/2007/04/02/107/

Hallinger, Philip, Leonard Bickman, and Ken Davis, "School Context, Principal Leadership, and Student Reading Achievement," *The Elementary School Journal*, Vol. 96, No. 5, 1996, pp. 527–549. As of October 18, 2009:
http://www.philiphallinger.com/papers/EAQ%20Leadership%20study%201996.pdf

Hallinger, Philip, and Ronald H. Heck, "Reassessing the Principal's Role in School Effectiveness: A Review of Empirical Research, 1980–1995," *Educational Administration Quarterly*, Vol. 32, No. 1, February 1996, pp. 5–44.

Hatch, Thomas, "When Improvement Programs Collide," *Phi Delta Kappan*, Vol. 83, No. 8, April 2002, pp. 626–634, 639.

Heck, Ronald H., Terry J. Larson, and George A. Marcoulides, "Instructional Leadership and School Achievement: Validation of a Causal Model," *Educational Administration Quarterly*, Vol. 26, No. 2, May 1990, pp. 94–125.

Hill, Peter W., "What Principals Need to Know About Teaching and Learning," in Marc S. Tucker and Judy B. Codding (eds.), *The Principal Challenge: Leading and Managing Schools in an Era of Accountability*, San Francisco, Calif.: Jossey-Bass Publishers, 2002, pp. 43–75.

Holland, Holly, *Out of the Office and into the Classroom: An Initiative to Help Principals Focus on Instruction*, New York: The Wallace Foundation, 2008. As of October 18, 2009:
http://www.wallacefoundation.org/SiteCollectionDocuments/WF/Knowledge%20Center/Attachments/PDF/stories-from-field-out-of-the-office.pdf

Honig, Meredith I., and Thomas C. Hatch, "Crafting Coherence: How Schools Strategically Manage Multiple, External Demands," *Educational Researcher*, Vol. 33, No. 8, 2004, pp. 16–30. As of October 18, 2009:
http://education.washington.edu/areas/edlps/profiles/faculty/papers/ER%20Honig%20and%20Hatch%202004.pdf

Hoyle, John R., Fenwick W. English, and Betty E. Steffy, *Skills for Successful 21st Century School Leaders: Standards for Peak Performers*, 3rd ed., Arlington, Va.: American Association of School Administrators, 1998.

Institute for Educational Leadership (IEL), *Leadership for Student Learning: Reinventing the Principalship*, a report of the Task Force on the Principalship, October 2000. As of October 18, 2009:
http://www.iel.org/programs/21st/reports/principal.pdf

Johnson, Jean, Ana Maria Arumi, and Amber Ott, *Reality Check 2006: Is Support for Standards and Testing Fading?* Public Agenda, 2006. As of October 18, 2009:
http://www.publicagenda.org/reports/reality-check-2006-issue-no-3

Knapp, Michael S., Michael A. Copland, Margaret L. Plecki, and Bradley S. Portin, *Leading, Learning, and Leadership Support*, Seattle, Wash.: Center for the Study of Teaching and Policy, University of Washington, October 2006.

Knapp, Michael S., Michael A. Copland, and Joan E. Talbert, *Leading for Learning: Reflective Tools for School and District Leaders*, Seattle, Wash.: Center for the Study of Teaching and Policy, University of Washington, February 2003.

Lane, B., and S. Gracia, "State-Level Support for Comprehensive School Reform: Implications for Policy and Practice," *Journal of Education for Students Placed at Risk*, Vol. 10, No.1, 2004, pp. 85–112.

Lashway, Larry, "Research Roundup: Rethinking the Principalship," *ERIC Clearinghouse on Educational Policy and Management*, Vol. 18, No. 3, 2002. As of October 18, 2009:
https://scholarsbank.uoregon.edu/xmlui/bitstream/handle/1794/3484/roundups_Spring_2002.pdf?sequence=1

Legler, Ray, and Thomas Reischl, "The Relationship of Key Factors in the Process of Collaboration: A Study of School-to-Work Coalitions," *Journal of Applied Behavioral Science*, Vol. 39, No. 1, March 2003, pp. 53–72.

Leithwood, Kenneth, Karen Seashore Louis, Stephen Anderson, and Kyla Wahlstrom, *How Leadership Influences Student Learning*, Minneapolis, Minn.: Center for Applied Research and Educational Improvement, University of Minnesota, September 2004.

Long, J. Scott, and Jeremy Freese, *Regression Models for Categorical Outcomes Using Stata*, 2nd ed., College Station, Tex.: Stata Press, 2005.

Lundin, Martin, "When Does Cooperation Improve Public Policy Implementation?" *The Policy Studies Journal*, Vol. 35, No. 4, 2007, pp. 629–652.

Madda, Christina L., Richard R. Halverson, and Louis M. Gomez, "Exploring Coherence as an Organizational Resource for Carrying Out Reform Initiatives," *Teachers College Record*, Vol. 109, No. 8, 2007, pp. 1957–1979.

Marks, Helen, and Susan Printy, "Principal Leadership and School Performance: An Integration of Transformational and Instructional Leadership," *Educational Administration Quarterly*, Vol. 39, No. 3, 2003, pp. 370–397.

May, Peter J., Joshua Sapotichne, and Samuel Workman, "Policy Coherence and Policy Domains," *Policy Studies Journal*, Vol. 34, No. 3, August 2006, pp. 381–403.

Mazzeo, Christopher, *Improving Teaching and Learning by Improving School Leadership*, Issue Brief, Washington, D.C.: National Governors Association Center for Best Practices, Educational Policy Studies Division, 2003. As of October 18, 2009: http://www.nga.org/Files/pdf/091203LEADERSHIP.pdf

McDonnell, Lorraine, "The Politics of Education: Influencing Policy and Beyond," in Susan H. Fuhrman, David K. Cohen, and Fritz Mosher (eds.), *The State of Education Policy Research*, Mahwah, N.J.: Lawrence Erlbaum Associates, 2007.

McGuire, Michael, "Collaborative Public Management: Assessing What We Know and How We Know It," *Public Administration Review*, Vol. 66, No. s1, December 2006, pp. 33–43.

Murphy, Joseph, "Reculturing Educational Leadership: The ISLLC Standards Ten Years Out," Vanderbilt University, paper prepared for the National Policy Board for Educational Administration, September 2003. As of October 18, 2009: http://www.npbea.org/Resources/ISLLC_10_years_9-03.pdf

Murphy, M., M. Martin, and R. Muth, "Partnerships for Preparing School Leaders: Possibilities and Practicalities," in R. Muth and M. Martin (eds.), *Toward the Year 2000: Leadership and Quality Schools. The Sixth Yearbook of the National Council of Professors of Educational Administration*, Lanham, Md.: Scarecrow Press, 1997, pp. 238–246.

National Center for Education Statistics (NCES), *NAEP Overview*, Jessup, Md.: U.S. Department of Education, Institute of Education Sciences, nd. As of October 16, 2009: http://nces.ed.gov/nationsreportcard/about/

National College for School Leadership (NCSL), *What We Know About School Leadership*, Nottingham, UK: National College for School Leadership, May 2007. As of October 18, 2009: http://www.nationalcollege.org.uk/docinfo?id=17480&filename=what-we-know-about-school-leadership.pdf

Newmann, Fred M., BetsAnn Smith, Elaine Allensworth, and Anthony S. Bryk, "Instructional Program Coherence: What It Is and Why It Should Guide School Improvement Policy," *Educational Evaluation and Policy Analysis*, Vol. 23, No. 4, 2001, pp. 297–321.

Norton, John, Kathy O'Neill, Betty Fry, and David Hill, "Universities in the Lead: Redesigning Leadership Preparation for Student Achievement," *SREB Leadership Newsletter*, Fall 2002, pp. 1–27.

Peterson, Kent D., "The Professional Development of Principals: Innovations and Opportunities," *Educational Administration Quarterly*, Vol. 38, No. 2, 2002, pp. 213–232.

Portin, Bradley, Paul Schneider, Michael DeArmond, and Lauren Gundlach, *Making Sense of Leading Schools: A Study of the School Principalship*, Seattle, Wash.: Center on Reinventing Public Education, University of Washington, September 2003. As of October 18, 2009: http://www.crpe.org/cs/crpe/view/csr_pubs/24

Provan, Keith G., and H. Brinton Milward, "A Preliminary Theory of Interorganizational Network Effectiveness: A Comparative Study of Four Community Mental Health Systems," *Administrative Science Quarterly*, Vol. 40, No. 1, March 1995, pp. 1–33.

Southern Regional Education Board (SREB), *Academies in the Lead: Redesigning Leadership Academies for Student Achievement*, newsletter, Atlanta, Ga.: SREB, 2003. As of October 18, 2009:
http://www.sreb.org/main/Leadership/pubs/03V59_Leadership_newsletter.pdf

———, *Schools Can't Wait: Accelerating the Redesign of University Preparation Programs*, Atlanta, Ga.: SREB, 2006. As of October 18, 2009:
http://www.sreb.org/programs/hstw/publications/special/06V04_Schools_Cant_Wait.pdf

Spillane, James P., "Cognition and Policy Implementation: District Policymakers and the Reform of Mathematics Education," *Cognition and Instruction*, Vol. 18, No. 2, 2000, pp. 141–179.

Tharp-Taylor, Shannah, Catherine Awsumb Nelson, Laura S. Hamilton, and Kun Yuan, *Pittsburgh Public Schools' Excellence for All Year 2 Evaluation*, Santa Monica, Calif.: RAND Corporation, DB-575-1-PPS, 2009. As of October 18, 2009:
http://www.rand.org/pubs/documented_briefings/DB575-1/

Thomson, Ann Marie, and James L. Perry, "Collaboration Processes: Inside the Black Box," *Public Administration Review*, Vol. 66, No. s1, December 2006, pp. 20–32. As of October 18, 2009:
http://www3.interscience.wiley.com/cgi-bin/fulltext/118561473/PDFSTART

Unger, Chris, Brett Lane, Elisabeth Cutler, Saeyun Lee, Joye Whitney, Elise Arruda, and Martin Silva, *How Can State Education Agencies Support District Improvement? A Conversation Amongst Educational Leaders, Researchers, and Policy Actors*, Providence, R.I.: The Education Alliance at Brown University, 2008.

Usdan, Michael, Barbara McCloud, and Mary Podmostko, *Leadership for Student Learning: Reinventing the Principalship*, Washington, D.C.: Institute for Educational Leadership, October 2000.

U.S. Department of Education, Institute of Education Sciences' National Center for Education Statistics, *Common Core of Data 2006–2007*. As of May 13, 2009:
http://nces.gov.ccd

Vitaska, Sarah, *Strong Leaders Strong Schools: 2007 State Laws*, Denver, Colo.: National Conference of State Legislatures, 2008.

The Wallace Foundation, "Wallace Launches Major State-District Initiative to Strengthen School Leadership," press release, January 8, 2002. As of October 18, 2009:
http://www.wallacefoundation.org/NewsRoom/PressRelease/Pages/1-8-02-DistrictState.aspx

———, *Leadership for Learning: Making the Connections Among State, District and School Policies and Practices*, New York, September 2006. As of October 18, 2009:
http://www.wallacefoundation.org/SiteCollectionDocuments/WF/Knowledge%20Center/Attachments/PDF/FINALWallaceCLSPerspective.pdf

Waters, Tim, Robert J. Marzano, and Brian McNulty, *Balanced Leadership: What 30 Years of Research Tells Us About the Effect of Leadership on Student Achievement*, Aurora, Colo.: Mid-Continent Research for Education and Learning, 2003.

Wirt, Frederick, and Michael Kirst, *Political Dynamics of American Education*, Richmond, Calif.: McCutchan Publishing Company, 1997.

Young, Michelle D., George J. Petersen, and Paula M. Short, "The Complexity of Substantive Reform: A Call for Interdependence Among Key Stakeholders," *Educational Administration Quarterly*, Vol. 38, No. 2, 2002, p. 137. As of October 18, 2009:
http://digitalcommons.calpoly.edu/cgi/viewcontent.cgi?article=1025&context=gse_fac